Spike Lee

"Lee will not be ingratiating; he wants to be accepted on his own rude terms."

Richard Schickel, film critic

"He's not a very good filmmaker, in my opinion. What he's trying to say, I think it's very ugly."

Alan Parker, director

"I think he really believes in revenge."

An anonymous colleague

"Kiss my ass, *two times!*"

Spike Lee

SPiKE LEE

ALEX PATTERSON

AVON BOOKS ◆ NEW YORK

All photographs are from Alex Patterson's personal collection unless
otherwise noted.

SPIKE LEE is an original publication of Avon Books. This work
has never before appeared in book form.

AVON BOOKS
A division of
The Hearst Corporation
1350 Avenue of the Americas
New York, New York 10019

Copyright © 1992 by Siegel and Siegel, Ltd.
Cover photographs by Rick McGinnis
This book is a creation of Siegel and Siegel, Ltd.
Library of Congress Catalog Card Number: 92-90327
ISBN: 0-380-76994-8

First Avon Books Printing: December 1992

AVON TRADEMARK REG. U.S. PAT. OFF. AND IN OTHER COUNTRIES, MARCA
REGISTRADA, HECHO EN U.S.A.

Printed in the U.S.A.

RA   10   9   8   7   6   5   4   3   2

Acknowledgments

Among those I'd like to thank for their assistance in the researching and writing of this book are:

Florence Anthony,
Chris Buck,
Tom Colgan,
Diana Elder,
First Run Pictures,
Rob Salem,
Shlomo Schwartzberg,
Barbara Siegel,
Scott Siegel,
Wayman Wong,

. . . and special thanks to Ron Goldberg, able assistant and all-round fine human being.

Contents

Foreword

In the early 1980s, a "Saturday Night Live" sketch had a host introducing a new arrival to his other guests at an up-scale cocktail party. One of those guests was played by black comic Garrett Morris. The host introduced Morris as a young actor who had just landed the lead role in a movie called *The Bill Cosby Story*.

"Congratulations," said the new guest. "But Bill Cosby is still alive—why doesn't he just play the part himself?"

"The studio felt it would be better," deadpanned Morris, "if the role were played by a black man."

The gag is still funny today. But in the intervening years, it has lost a lot of its relevance. Many factors helped bring about this change. One of the most significant of these factors goes by the name of Spike

Lee. Because of Spike, black moviemaking will never be the same.

The term "overnight success" may be a cliché. But in the case of Spike Lee, it really does apply: not overnight *sensation*; overnight *success*. "Overnight sensation" implies that a person won't be around long—a flash in the pan. "Overnight *success*," on the other hand, just means that person made a very big impression in a very short period of time. Spike Lee arrived a ready-made news item. He's been a major celebrity ever since.

He has been called "America's most controversial director." At least on that count, there can be little debate. Many Blacks idolize him, seeing in his movies the eloquent expression of their frustrations. Many Whites fear and loathe him, seeing in those same movies the potential for black revolution. He's a one man vigilante committee. He's also a savvy media manipulator and a one-man industry. And he's not about to go away.

But it wasn't always like this. Exploding onto the scene in late 1986, Spike Lee was just a young man living in a basement apartment in Brooklyn. Armed with a camera, an attitude and a vanload of ambition, he was determined to make his mark on the world. When *She's Gotta Have It* was unleashed on an unsuspecting public, few could have predicted that, within five years, the diminutive B-boy with the gold MARS nameplate around his neck would be an African-American hero—let alone one of the most famous people in the world. You could see that he was headed for *something,* but I doubt if even the self-assured Spike expected that he'd become a household name.

Other celebrities get themselves in the news by dint of where they go or with whom they have sex. Certain celebs, in fact, are *more* famous for who they've been seen with than for their own work. Not so Spike. Despite being an eminently desirable bachelor, Spike keeps his private life private. With most stars, biographers concentrate on their subject's private lives: such things as their ex-husbands, future-wives, onetime sex partners. In the case of Spike Lee, what's far more interesting is who he *fights* with: that list indeed constitutes a veritable Who's Who of important journalists, movie stars and prominent politicians.

Like Spike, I spent my teens at "quality films" from Europe, Japan and the fringes of the United States. Unlike Spike, however, I was also a fan of the great Blaxploitation flicks of the 1970s. As a white teenager in a clean, crime-free Canadian suburb, movies like *Shaft, Superfly* and *Across 110th Street* (and the novels of Chester Himes) offered excitement, intrigue and macho heroics so far from my experience that they might have been from another planet. Yet there was clearly more attracting me than just action: James Bond never really turned my crank, and Charles Bronson I could live without. But Richard Roundtree or Ron O'Neal chasing enemies through Harlem's derelict tenements, vacant lots and garbage-strewn alleys—now *there* was excitement. Some of the political themes of these movies went right over my teenaged head, but the message of racial pride came through loud and clear.

It's nothing new for white kids to look up to black heroes. From Jackie Robinson to Eddie Murphy, American Blacks have risen to the heights of sports and entertainment—so long as they don't get too uppity on racial matters. But for Whites to appreciate Blacks who have strong, uncomfortable things to say about blackness, well, that's a more recent phenomenon. Spike Lee (and John Singleton and Matty Rich and Public Enemy) have, from the beginning, been uncompromising in their racial politics and have been proudly, defiantly black. That they should appeal to a black constituency is no surprise: African-Americans are clearly in need of more honest representations of themselves on screens and over the airwaves. That such politically charged, even angry, work should also be of interest to white audiences, however, is something new.

At college, Spike Lee once made a student film to counter the flagrant racism of D. W. Griffith's *Birth of a Nation*. I, too, had a growth experience as a result of that troublesome classic. Catching it in someone else's film class, I was simultaneously intrigued by its technique and infuriated by its message. How could a supposedly responsible institution show this blatant redneck propaganda without so much as a word from the instructor to place its odious politics in historical context? I hastily scribbled several hundred words excoriating the film department—*not* for showing the film, but for showing it without some sort of preface to defuse its white supremacist message. Not knowing quite what to do with my little manifesto, I took it to the editor of the college paper. The editor pointed out that, as the paper covered only new releases, a silent movie from 1915 wasn't really current enough. "But," he said, "you seem to be able to write about movies, so maybe you'd like to be our critic." That afternoon put an untimely end to my proposed career of watching rats run through mazes.

When *She's Gotta Have It* hit the screen in late 1986, I was a free-lance film critic in Toronto. Always interested in viewing exciting new work and fresh insights, I attended and liked what I saw. Since then, the hard-working Spike has sent us films at a rate of almost one per year: *School Daze* (1988), *Do the Right Thing* (1989), *Mo' Better Blues* (1990), *Jungle Fever* (1991) and *Malcolm X* (1992). Each one has been controversial; each one has been a hit with audiences. Collectively, they have raised Spike's profile to where he can't walk a city block without being mobbed for autographs—or yelled at for past sins, real or imagined.

"I'm black," Spike Lee told the *New York Times* at the time of *Do the Right Thing*'s release in 1989. "It's a fact. Like saying the sky is blue. Am I bitter about it? No. Am I angry about it? No. Am I aware of what it means to be black in America today? Yes."

I'm white. It's a fact. It's like saying grass is green. Do I feel superior about it? No. Do I hold offensive views about Blacks because of it? No. Am I aware of what it means to be black in America today? Well, maybe not. But I'm trying. I know that no White can ever *really* know what it means to be a different color—no, not even with the *Black Like Me* shoe-polish treatment. But, contrary to what some racial radicals proclaim, there *are* a few of us out there who recognize the seriousness of the situation and would like to make some small contribution to improving it.

Now that Spike Lee has taken his place among the foremost living American film directors, some assessment of his life and career is in order. Neither his life nor his career is without faults—some of them glaring. Even so, Spike Lee is an original, individual talent worthy of serious critical examination.

More than any other director, there is little or no distance between Spike's views and Spike's films. "That they *are* his views is unmistakable," wrote Michael Wilmington in the November 1991 *L.A. Style*. "More than any other black filmmaker, past or present, Lee has made his films into his own spiritual, emotional and intellectual autobiography, tearing himself open and putting the world within and oustide him on public display." What you see is what he believes, with no ironic distancing allowed. For this reason, Spike can be analyzed through his movies to an extent that would simply be impossible with more contradictory artists like, say, Martin Scorsese or Spike's old nemesis, Steven Spielberg. With Spike, you at least know where you stand. He has, since Day One, been almost painfully explicit and plain, both in his movies and in interviews (and, having given thousands, he is one of the most frequently interviewed people in America).

This is not to say that some of those works and his words have not been misunderstood. "He sometimes seems suspicious of the best-intentioned criticism," wrote Donna Britt in the *Washington Post,* June 30, 1989. When I mentioned that Spike seems "unusually sensitive to being criticized" to a New York editor, she was quick to disagree, arguing that Spike was no worse than average about that, and in some ways better. The difference, she felt, was that when Spike was displeased with someone, he'd tell them in no uncertain terms. Other movie people, she explained, wouldn't let you know anything was wrong—until, of course, you found yourself shut out of a screening of their next film. Spike's prickly-but-honest approach, she felt, was preferable to the genteel backstabbing of Hollywood custom.

Spike Lee declined to be interviewed for this book. This is, after all, the first book that has been published about him not to have come from his own pen, and Spike is someone who likes to keep a close control over things. The following quote from *Woody Allen: A Biography* (Knopf, 1991) by Eric Lax should illustrate what this book is not: "There were really two Allan Konigsbergs at Midwood High. There was the shy boy who in most instances said nothing and whom hardly anyone recognized. And there was the Allan Konigsberg with Woody Allen bursting out him who showed his brilliance to pockets of people." (p. 141–42)

This book contains no armchair-psychologist blather like the above.

One last item: When it comes to capitalizing names of races, book publishers, magazines and newspapers all have their own policies and house styles. Some capitalize "White" but not "black"; others (including Spike Lee's books) capitalize "Black" but not "white." Aiming to be fair—and grammatically correct—this book capitalizes both "Black" and "White" when they are used as nouns. When they are used as adjectives, they are set in lower case.

Chapter 1

"Spikey":
The Talented Tenth

The man we know as "Spike" was born Shelton
Jackson Lee on March 20, 1957 in Atlanta, Georgia.
The first of five children, he got the nickname Spike
from his mother, Jacquelyn Lee—a fitting tribute to
what Jacquelyn always said was "a tough baby."
Apparently Spike's tendency to be difficult is one
that goes right back to the crib. The infant Spike,
much like the man he grew into, was small but loud.

The family into which he was born was extraordinary for a number of reasons. His parents, college-
educated newlyweds, each came from families that
stressed both creativity and black tradition. Spike's
jazz musician father Bill Lee had been born in 1929
in Snow Hill, Alabama. A small, mostly black, agri-
cultural area, Snow Hill is situated a mere seventeen
miles from Selma, where some of the most famous
civil rights fights were fought. Snow Hill's success
and survival as a community seemed to depend on

having as little to do with the white world outside it as it could possibly manage. In such an environment, without worries about pleasing and appeasing the white folks, families like Bill Lee's could concentrate on their own heritage. Bill's father, the son of the early black educator William James Edwards, had also had the good fortune to be born to folks who cared about where they came from.

Toward the end of the last century, Bill Lee's esteemed grandfather (and namesake), William James Edwards, attended Alabama's Tuskegee Institute, one of the nation's first organizations devoted to educating and uplifting Blacks. Edwards put into action Tuskegee's motto, "Cast your buckets down where you are"—a powerful metaphor for educated and/or lucky Blacks to return to their communities and help others less fortunate than themselves. In 1893, Edwards established a school of his own when he founded what is now known as the Snow Hill Institute. Snow Hill and its spirit of self-improvement have exerted an influence on several generations of Lees: Spike's aunt Consuela, who worked with Bill Lee on the music for *School Daze*, began her choir there. Years later, Spike's talented photographer brother David would document the town in words and pictures in the book *Snow Hill, Ala*.

A turning point in the life of Malcolm X was when, as a seventh grade student in Michigan, his (white) teacher told young Malcolm Little that his dream of becoming a lawyer was an unrealistic goal for a Negro. The Lee family, however, has never been vulnerable to such thwarting of their ambition or accepting of outwardly imposed limitations on their potential. Even so, Bill Lee didn't see much of a future for himself or his young family in the American South of the 1950s. After all, Spike was born only a matter of months after Rosa Parks began the Montgomery, Alabama, bus strike by refusing to give up her seat. "Civil rights" was still a whisper, though it would soon be a scream. At the age of thirty, with talent, a little money and a young child, Mr. Lee decided to take his clan north.

Their first stop was Chicago, where Bill Lee knew some musicians. More of a center for blues than for jazz, Chicago proved to be not quite what Lee was looking for. In what was to become their final resting place, the family then packed up and trekked east to Union Street, in the Crown Heights section of what Spike likes to call "the great borough of Brooklyn, New York."

The year was 1959, and New York City was the jazz capital of the world. Greenwich Village was alive with the sounds of hot, stompin' trios, quartets, quintets and orchestras. Bill Lee, a solid, reliable bassman, could find work both in clubs and as a session player in the studio. Jazz—"the original African-American art form," as Spike's film *Mo' Better Blues* would later assert—has always been Bill Lee's first love. But playing jazz is a tough way to make a living even for those at the very top of the profession. And, although Bill had no way of knowing it, the widespread acceptance of his music had already reached its peak. The tastes of the white Beat generation kids of the 1950s would soon give way to the folk music craze of the early 1960s, and jazz would never again enjoy such widespread acceptance outside its diehard followers.

Although Bill preferred the longer, more improvisatory modes of the jazz idiom, he was still flexible enough to lend his talents to the emerging generation of neo-folkies. Mr. Lee paid the rent many a month with session work on albums by then popular folk acts Judy Collins, Bob Dylan, Peter, Paul and Mary, and Simon and Garfunkel. But there was one rule that Lee would not cross, having to do not with genre but with instrumentation: to this day, Bill Lee is known as a man who plays only acoustic bass. Bill is among the acoustic hardliners (pianist Keith Jarrett is another) who believe that electrification irreversibly distorts the purity of tone, representing a trend of the modern world that is to be strenuously resisted.

But the tides of time were against him on this one. After Bob Dylan "went electric"—and turned the trend from folk to folk-rock—in the middle of that tumultuous decade, Bill Lee found his services required by fewer and fewer employers. His defiant decision not to abandon his artistic standards pretty much put him out of work thereafter. To this day, the Fender electric bass is a contraption Bill Lee will not touch. Luckily for him—and his young children—Bill Lee had a sympathetic wife. "When he stopped working," Spike told *Vanity Fair*, "my mother became the sole breadwinner of our family."

Jacquelyn Shelton, a native of Atlanta, went to Spelman College, which, along with its brother school, Morehouse, was a black liberal arts college in Atlanta. (Spike's sister Joie would later attend Spelman, too.) Bill Lee met his future wife in 1951, his senior year. On Sundays, the Morehouse cafeteria was closed, leaving the men to fend for themselves, and leading Bill to seek Sunday dinner from

Jackie's mother, Zimmie Shelton. Jackie had come from a family that, similar to Bill's, stressed black pride and education. Zimmie Shelton, for instance, had always been disturbed by how hard it was to find products that reflected the black experience. To make sure her only daughter saw some reflections, Mrs. Shelton would go out of her way to track down black dolls for her—even though those early ones she found were both unattractive and unlifelike. She would even sit at her kitchen table with a fine-haired brush and some brown watercolor paint, adding some much-needed pigmentation to the pasty faces of that lily-white era's greeting cards and books. This atmosphere of proud (but non-fanatical) race consciousness was recreated by Bill and Jackie Lee in the home in which Spike Lee was formed.

Mrs. Lee, a pretty, bright and lively woman, was an art teacher at St. Ann's School in Brooklyn Heights. As a teacher, Jacquelyn naturally prodded the growing Spike to do well in school. Yet Spike, despite his clear intellectual abilities and slightly above average grades, was not an exceptional student. In his book *Spike Lee's Gotta Have It* Spike assesses his own abilities as merely mediocre, lacking much in the way of devotion to schoolwork, doing "just good enough to get by."

Still, his mother made sure he got a good education one way or another: Mrs. Lee would frequently take her son to museums, movies and the theater. Spike particularly remembers being frightened even to the point of tears by all the singing, dancing and other commotion at a Broadway performance of *The King and I*. But the boy got over it enough to develop a taste for music—and even for musicals—that would eventually figure in his creation of *School Daze*.

Over the next few years, the infant Spike would be joined by a younger sister Joie, and three brothers: David, Chris and Cinque. Bill and (especially) Jackie made sure that their children were well provided for not only materially but also spiritually and culturally. In particular, the parents were strong on instilling in their children the importance of the remarkable history their family had lived in the South—both by telling stories around the house and by showing the children the actual people and places on summer trips. Despite the logistical nightmares of a family of seven traveling by car, every summer Bill and Jackie Lee would load up the Citroën station wagon and head to either Snow Hill, Alabama, or Atlanta, Georgia, to spend time with the grandparents.

One of the most influential residences of Spike's formative years was a well-kept town house at 186 Warren Street in Cobble Hill. Predominantly Jewish, Cobble Hill is one of Brooklyn's cleanest, prettiest neighborhoods—and one of very few with much in the way of racial integration. "We were the first Blacks in that neighborhood," says Spike in *Spike Lee's Gotta Have It*, though he claims they "didn't have any problems" with acceptance. Their Jewish neighbors Spike remembers as having been more "tolerant" than the Italian-Americans they had lived around in the past. Curiously, the "tolerant" Jews have come in for just as harsh a portrayal as the less tolerant Italian-Americans in his films. Like his fellow Northerner Malcolm X, Spike was surrounded by white people as he came of age— unlike his father and Martin Luther King, Jr., for whom other Southern Blacks were the norm.

Later, his parents bought the house at 165 Washington Park, Fort Greene, where Bill Lee still lives today with his second wife, Susan Kaplan. At that time, Fort Greene was a somewhat rough area, but Mr. and Mrs. Lee felt it was worth taking a small step down socially in order to own their own property. Today, Fort Greene is rapidly becoming Brooklyn's Buppie headquarters, its "comeback" due in no small measure to Spike himself. The director has become something of a Fort Greene real estate mogul, turning a real estate office into his memorabilia store, a fire station into a filmworks, and acquiring other film-related facilities in close proximity.

Spike is Fort Greene's favorite son, a local hero recognized by all and mobbed for autographs. Despite his independent financial status that allows him to live almost anywhere he pleases, he has never wanted to leave (although he does now own a summer home in exclusive Martha's Vineyard). Never having learned to drive, Spike appreciates having everything close by, and can still be seen buying newspapers in corner shops and even riding the subway. More often, though, he now travels by chauffeured limousine or in cars with friends at the wheel.

Because of all these signifiers of class—the Citroëns, the private schools, the Broadway shows—it has been suggested that Spike's B-boy image is a pose, or at least an exaggeration. Some people get suspicious when Spike employs "gonna" and "gotta" in his speech and even in his written works. Yet he's also capable of coming up with ornate, convoluted sentences in structures suggesting a much more bourgeois background. The intelligent content of his speech is often undermined by double negatives ("didn't like no music"), misaligned verbs ("they be"), and other semiliterate signifiers of, in the words of a character in *She's Gotta Have It,* "ignorant ghetto Negroes."

"People have this impression that we came from an upper-class upbringing because we had a Citroën car and three kids went to private school," sister Joie Lee told *Spy* magazine. (Citroëns, no longer exported to the United States, were eccentric French luxury sedans favored by intellectuals and artists.)

"I went to public school," Spike stressed to *Playboy.* "My brother Chris went to public school. But David, Joie and Cinque went to private school. I always could tell a difference in them because they went to private school. Their negritude got honed or harnessed going into these predominantly white private schools. They know it. Most of their friends were white. Not that I have anything against that, it's just that there is definitely an argument for being around your own people."

The Lees were certainly better off than the typical black family, but they weren't the Huxtables, either. Being a jazz musician brings status, but rarely the rent. There were many times when their phone was cut off for nonpayment.

Yet Spike regularly gives credit for his successes to the stability that comes from having a close-knit, two-parent family and knowing one's family tree—especially one as outstanding as Spike's. These intangibles undoubtedly did more to ensure that Spike would grow up to be someone special than did his clan's (somewhat) elevated social status.

Of the neighborhood itself, Spike insisted in a *Playboy* interview, "There were never any gangs. I don't remember ever seeing any. There were people who would steal your lunch money, that wasn't no gang thing. I mean, now they'll shoot you up. When I was growing up, they might take a quarter from you. You give it up . . . but it's not like 'Give us your leather coat or I'll shoot you.' "

Is the star's public image hiding a privileged upbringing? Is he a hypocrite, a fake? No. The truth is that Spike Lee is a product of contradictions: both B-boy and Buppie, both the kid from the street and the college boy. If he goes out of his way to use current urban slang ("down," "slammin' "), it's just his way of showing solidarity with current black culture.

In *Playboy*, Spike himself has confronted the myth that the only *real* Blacks are poor Blacks—a notion brimming with potential for self-destruction. "There's something very sick where if you speak well and you speak articulately, that's looked at as being negative and speaking white. I remember when I was growing up, people used to tell me, 'You sound white.' I've been reading of various cases where kids flunk on purpose so they'll be considered 'down' with the home boys and stuff. That's crazy when intelligence is thought of as being white and all the other stuff is being black and being down. I think that one has to be able to navigate both worlds. You ought to be able to speak with your brothers on the street but at the same time be able to go to a job inter-view, fill out the application and speak proper English."

At various times, Spike Lee attended P.S. 29, P.S. 7 and P.S. 8, and then Rothschild (now Public Junior High School 294). The school which had the most impact on him, however, was John Dewey High School in Coney Island, a "special" high school with a flexible curriculum in which students determined their own studies. After he graduated in the summer of 1975, he went directly to Morehouse College.

He played some sports—softball and basketball—often as team captain. Friends remember him getting as much enjoyment from the organizing as from the playing of the games. Spike's other main form of recreation was going to movies. But while most of his contemporaries were into Blaxploitation or kung fu epics at Times Square grindhouses, Spike attended foreign fare and what he likes to call "quality films" at art houses. The grown-up Spike dismisses the low-budget Jim Brown-Fred Williamson thrillers of the seventies: "I hate that Blaxploitation shit, never went to it." (He does, however, admit to seeing Bruce Lee's *Enter the Dragon*.)

Spike attributes his "difference" to an unusually artistic family that always had music around the house—jazz, mostly, but also R&B. Spike preferred R&B to jazz, much to his father's dismay. In fact, his taste in music was his way of rejecting his parents' authority. Going into film instead of music might have been, too. "I probably could have followed in my father's footstep," said Spike in the *Mo' Better* book, "but I rebelled against it. He never pushed me into it, not any of his children. Whatever we wanted to do with our lives was fine with him." What began as a simple teenage attitude problem turned out to be music's loss and film's gain.

But his love for music always ran a poor second to his passion for movies. Spike recalls his "Moms" taking him to *Bye Bye Birdie*, *A Hard Day's Night* (though Papa Bill forbade the Beatles and other non-jazz around the household) and James Bond movies—mainstream moviegoing for the sixties. And Dad would let him tag along to some of his gigs at the Blue Note and other jazz landmarks.

Art and race: these twin themes of culture and racial pride ran through both the Lees and the Sheltons converging in their first offspring. Spike would later unite them in ways that would bring about unprecedented popular acceptance. Morehouse alumni remember how Spike got in a famous fracas over how the homecoming queens should dress. Spike felt that, by expecting them to parade in revealing costumes, his college fellows were dissing their females. Spike wanted them to be more dignified, like real African queens—a confrontation that ended with the girls putting on some more clothes. And one that would later be transmuted into art in *School Daze,* in a scene in which politics (this time racial, not sexual) interrupts another homecoming parade.

Spike's earliest attempts at expressing himself were at Morehouse, on a radio show at campus station WCLK where he played jazz and soul music, and writing for the school newspaper. While at Morehouse, Spike also wrote his first short film, *Black College: The Talented Tenth*—a virtually suppressed project of which Spike seems profoundly embarrassed. (The title refers to the black bourgoisie, the minority within the community who have overcome prejudice and succeeded in the white world.)

Spike is justifiably proud of being a third-generation Morehouse grad. His father has reminisced about how his own big-man-on-campus status evaporated as soon as he left the college grounds: he would be barred from many restaurants, be required to ride in the back of the bus—and always be at risk of random redneck violence. The difference in Morehouse experiences between father (1947–51) and son (1975–79) was profound—an improvement Papa credits to "the work of one man, Martin Luther King, Jr." Another proud Morehouse alumnus, Dr. King was a senior there when Bill Lee was a junior. (Bill Cosby is yet another distinguished Morehouse man.)

By the time Spike was matriculating in the late seventies, Georgia may still not have been the best place in the world to be Black, but it was infinitely better than the American apartheid his father had faced in the bad old days of segregation and colored-only drinking fountains. And it was at Morehouse that Spike met Monty Ross, his future coproducer, right-hand man and best friend. Morehouse also introduced Spike to Pamm Jackson, his production designer Wyn Thomas, and Rolanda Watts, who went on to become a New York TV reporter.

Spike's mother, whom he still adored, wrote him long letters when he first went away to college. When he wrote back, she corrected his grammar with a red magic marker. Unfortunately, Jacquelyn Lee was by this time already quite ill with cancer of the liver. In October of 1976, when Spike was

nineteen years old and had just begun his sophomore
year at Morehouse, Mrs. Lee suddenly took a turn for
the worse and passed away.

Spike was devastated. Years later he would tell
Vanity Fair that he still reads and re-reads those
letters. And he still dreams about her at night, sometimes waking to tell Zimmie, "Mama, I could *feel* her
there." Zimmie had always felt that her daughter had
mothered Spike just a little too much. "Let him be a
child," she used to tell Jackie, over and over.

His maternal grandmother, Zimmie Shelton, took
his mother's place in Spike's life. Spike calls her
Mama to this day and keeps a closer, less fractious
relationship with her than with his own father.
Zimmie, born in 1907, is now a very old lady,
rarely traveling outside Atlanta—or even to see her
own grandson's hit movies. She recalls seeing one,
but isn't sure which one. (It was *She's Gotta Have
It*. Spike has described Zimmie's review as positive,
despite the graphic sex scenes. As a strict Baptist, it
was the cursing Mrs. Shelton objected to.)

Part of his closeness with his grandmother
unquestionably came from his mother's death, but
it was also due in part to his growing conflicts
with his father—which went beyond the expected
levels of adolescent rebellion. It's not uncommon
for teenagers to experiment with drugs and for their
parents to react with disapproval and disgust. In the
Lee family, it was the other way around.

Growing up, Spike never touched marijuana or
other drugs. He had friends who smoked dope, he
says, although most did not. He never even developed a taste for beer until well into his twenties,
and to this day his alcohol intake is little to none.

Nowadays, Spike reflects, with the widespread use of harder drugs, parents "pray to God that's *all* your child is doing is smoking marijuana." (The mind reels at how much young black talent may be wiped out by vicious, addictive drugs like crack cocaine that are now available on street corners and in schoolyards before such talent even gets the chance to show itself.)

Spike's stringent avoidance of all drugs was undoubtedly influenced by his father. Being in music, Bill Lee had always been around drugs and had sampled various kinds over the years. Around 1970, however, he began to experiment with heroin. What worsened the situation was his wife's death—which, of course, was when Spike was off at college and unable to keep an eye on the situation. Bill Lee seems always to have been a fairly low-level user—not that there's really any such thing as "a manageable habit" where needles are concerned. There's nothing new or surprising about jazz musicians using drugs, though the ones who graduate from soft drugs to needles usually don't live as long as Bill Lee has done. They don't usually stay out of trouble with the law very long, either. Yet Bill Lee carried on unchallenged until 1991, when he was busted trying to buy heroin in Fort Greene's Washington Park.

When Spike went south to Morehouse in 1975, he sported a then-fashionable "massive Tito Jackson 'fro," according to the teasing of his younger brother David. He has always looked young for his age—which he does to this day, an advantage that still permits him to get away with things like playing *Do the Right Thing*'s twentyish Mookie when he was thirty-one. As a Morehouse freshman, however, it was not a plus: looking like a high-school kid surrounded by thousands of college men is not the way to impress girls. Still, Spike has never been one to settle for a low profile. He now applied his old leadership qualities from the schoolyard to organizing homecoming pageants—which tended to be very colorful affairs, with students riding bicycles on the stage, dressed in elaborate and imaginative costumes.

It was also at Morehouse that Spike began to discover that his real interest was in filmmaking—a hobby that was to become his life's work—while playing with hand-held Super-8 cameras borrowed from the school's audio-visual department. He and Monty Ross both became infected with the idea that it was up to the two of them to right the wrongs the silver screen had done Blacks since the invention of celluloid. According to a friend, Spike didn't just want to get into the House of Hollywood, he wanted to rearrange the furniture and then go out and publicize the password. That is, he wanted to rewrite the rules not only for himself, but for all his talented young contemporaries for whom the traditional studio system was not laying out a welcome mat. Spike recognized that there were many others like him who had many things to say—and the talent with which to say it—but felt stuck on the sidelines of a white-controlled power structure. The answer, Spike and Monty soon realized, was to beat Tinseltown at its own game.

Spike, in his way, carries on his ancestors' bucket-casting by making movies addressed to an audience the entertainment establishment has customarily ignored. Whether he practices this uplift enough is a matter for debate: some of his critics accuse him of being less interested in what's good for the race than in what's good for Spike Lee. To his credit, however, Spike has initiated scholarships for young black filmmakers and contributed to many charities and causes. Spike certainly leaves himself open to much justifiable criticism, but he also gets a lot that is *un*justifiable.

"I've had a competitive spirit since I was very young," Spike told *Playboy*. This spirit also had an effect on his siblings, each of whom have gone on to interesting careers themselves. His younger sister Joie and brother Cinque are now both actors, and David is a photographer. Chris, the "forgotten" Lee, was for a while a resident of Washington, D.C., and is currently working in his more famous brother's Fort Greene clothing store, Spike's Joint.

None has gone on to become a professional jazz musician.

Chapter 2

1982–84:
Straight Back to Brooklyn

*The emotions that accompany white attitudes
toward the Negro run a gamut including affection, kindliness, pity, indulgence, fear, hostility.
The one thing no white man will overtly give a
Negro is respect. . . . Nothing the White offers
to the Negro is more significant in shaping the
relations of the two races, than the respect he
withholds.*

—HORTENSE POWDERMAKER, *After Freedom*
(a 1939 anthropological study of Cottonville,
Mississippi)

Black students often remark on how refreshing they
find going to a black college and being among the
company of their peers for the first time after living
in a white world all their lives. So it was with Spike
Lee. However, although his memories of Morehouse

were mostly fond ones, he still preferred the North to the South. And having his appetite for film whetted but not satisfied at Morehouse, he knew he wasn't through with education. But no black college offered what Spike knew he needed: practical filmmaking instruction at a very advanced level. UCLA and USC were both out: Spike said, "I don't drive," and that was that.

In order to satisfy his different wants and needs, only one place would do: the acclaimed Cinema Studies program at New York University, home of his idol Martin Scorsese. In the *Spike Lee's Gotta Have It* book he says "I truly feel I was meant to be a filmmaker." And it was at NYU that he learned how.

Spike quietly went about the business of learning what he needed to learn. Like many film students, he found the school less useful for what it taught than for the availability of its equipment. Spike knew what he really wanted to do was not to talk about other people's movies, but to get his hands on some cameras and lights and make his own. When he gained access to the college's audio-visual department, Spike opened Pandora's box. Inside, he found *The Answer*.

On the subject of a black screenwriter hired by Hollywood to write the script for a $50 million remake of *Birth of a Nation*—D. W. Griffith's cinematically innovative but notoriously racist classic of the silent cinema—*The Answer* was an open provocation. Spike even included clips from *Birth* itself, which his teachers apparently saw as an act of unforgivable insubordination. D. W. Griffith was unquestionably a great technical pioneer and *Birth of a Nation* a groundbreaking picture in its story-telling methods. It also happens to be one of the most hateful pieces of white supremacist propaganda ever to masquerade as popular entertainment. Spike is entirely justified in reviving the NAACP's famous 1915 protest against *Birth*'s Negro villains and heroic Ku Klux Klan lynch mob, and to remind us that "Black men were lynched because of that film." (And, lest we forget, the novel on which *Birth of a Nation* was based was called *The Clansman*.) So, if ever a classic film was ripe for revisionist irreverence, *Birth of a Nation* is it. *The Answer* is a film Spike continues to defend. The NYU administration, however, tells a different story, arguing that their objection to *The Answer* was not its dissing of the great god Griffith, but its lack of coherence and artistry.

But Spike did more at grad school. It was there that he met another of the most important people in his life, cinematographer Ernest Dickerson. Dickerson, a Howard graduate, completed the power trio Spike began with Monty Ross back at Morehouse. Other NYU students remember Spike Lee as someone who was always extremely focused on his work and his vision. Spike, they recall, associated with Dickerson, but few others. "He was the nerd who studied hard and made good," says one. "I admire him because he knew exactly what he wanted and went out and got it." No one who knows him, friend or foe, denies that Spike Lee is a hard worker: "24–7–365" (twenty-four hours a day, seven days a week, 365 days a year) is how Spike likes to put it.

In particular, one incident at NYU is noteworthy,

if not for being typical then at least for being very, very strange. Near the end of one semester, a class discussion of the various students' films was held. One young man had made a film in which he played his part in drag. Spike seemed unable to discuss any other aspect of the film. "Obviously," Spike theorized, "you did this because you're homosexual." There was no malice in Spike's voice, but he was insistent just the same.

"No, I'm not," said his classmate. "I'm heterosexual. I just wanted to do this in women's clothes."

But Spike had made up his mind and wasn't about to listen. "No, you're obviously homosexual. That's why you played your part in women's clothes."

Again, the other student protested: "Look, I'm telling you, I'm *not* homosexual," and so on.

It was not so much that Spike was being homophobic as stubborn: the role he had mysteriously chosen was not that of an anti-gay bigot but that of psychoanalyst. What this suggests about Spike is something that has been borne out by the ensuing years: once he's made up his mind about something, there's no use trying to change it—even if what he's decided is flagrantly illogical.

In his second year at NYU, Dickerson shot Spike's second short, *Sarah,* a sentimental drama about a Harlem Thanksgiving. Generally considered the least of his early works, *Sarah* has been largely forgotten because of the provocation of the earlier *Answer* and the excellence of the later *Joe's Bed-Stuy Barbershop: We Cut Heads.*

At NYU, "I had to prove whether I belonged or was just another quota," Spike says in the *Gotta Have It* book. Any worries he or anyone else may have had on that count were put to rest by *Joe's Bed-Stuy Barbershop*. Spike chose a barbershop setting because it is, he says, "second only in importance to the church in the black community" as a place for folks to gather and talk.

Joe's Bed-Stuy was made in his senior year at NYU and is Spike's first film of real significance. A one-hour drama, it was shot (in color) by Ernest Dickerson and stars the director's future co-producer and right-hand man, Monty Ross.

The $13,000 *Joe's* cost may sound modest—except that it had to come mostly out of the filmmaker's own pockets. Film schools may provide the gear and donate some short-ends or other raw stock, but the rest of the expenses are up to the student. For some students, of course, this is not a problem; in 1992, Spike still recalls with some resentment that his film was judged against those by rich kids who spent upwards of $150,000 of the family fortune on their term project. (Christopher Guest's underrated 1989 Hollywood comedy *The Big Picture* does a good job of satirizing such big-budget, small-talent student films.) In Spike's case, financial assistance was provided not by a trust fund but by his beloved grandmother, Zimmie Shelton, whom he thanked by listing her as producer in the credits.

Joe's Bed-Stuy Barbershop: We Cut Heads won the student Academy Award for 1983. It also played the New Directors/New Films series—the first student film ever invited to do so—and was shown on selected Public Broadcasting System stations. Yet contrary to popular myth, this did *not* mean that Spike immediately became the industry's hottest young director, and Hollywood did *not* come hammering at his door. "I got to go to a couple of film festivals around the world, and I ended up with ICM and William Morris [talent agencies] for a cup of coffee," Spike recalled in *Gotta Have It*. "But they were unable to generate me any work, not even an after-school special. So that just cemented in my mind what I always thought all along: that I would have to go out and do it alone, not rely on anyone else."

At this point in his career, Spike Lee had not yet established enough of a reputation that anyone in the business would call him up to offer work. He had to make things happen for himself—even doing things "on spec" if necessary. Seeing music-video directors going on to make features, Spike decided that doing a video might be a way to establish his credentials. He would do something radical and daring: invest his own money in a video shoot, with no guarantee that what he made would be used. The track Spike chose to illustrate was a good one: Grandmaster Flash and the Furious Five's anti-cocaine anthem, "White Lines"—not only a landmark in hip-hop but one of the most dynamic tracks of the 1980s.

Despite claiming to like Spike's work, Grandmaster Flash's record company, Sugarhill Records, decided to pass on it. This left Spike and company with an impressive résumé item, but otherwise financially out of pocket. And this was not a man with money to lose: he still held down a day job, cleaning film at a lab for the chump change of $200 a week.

Ernest Dickerson was doing a little better, landing gigs like shooting *Krush Groove* as well as *The Brother from Another Planet* and the popular Bruce

Springsteen video for "Born in the USA," both for director John Sayles.

Then Spike came up with the idea for his first low-budget, independently financed, full-length movie. It was to be a comedy-drama, and it was to be called *The Messenger*. And it was to be the worst experience of Spike's young life.

Never finished, *The Messenger* (no relation to the Muslim newspaper of the same name) began and ended in the summer of 1984. About a bicycle courier and his interracial family in Brooklyn, the script was more than a little autobiographical: Bill Lee had remarried a white woman named Susan Kaplan a few years after his wife's death, a woman with whom Spike has had strained relations over the years. *The Messenger* is a title with metaphorical implications if ever there was one. The trend toward the painfully obvious continues in the plot, in which the protagonist drives the evil white bitch out of the family home—violently—in a resolution so blatant and so cheap that it resembles one of Homey the Clown's reverse-racist revenge fantasies on *In Living Color,* in which Homey kicks the butt of the snotty maitre d' Monsoor Snowflake.

Spike's first full-length project was aborted after he got in over his head financially. Not even a guarantee of $20,000 from the Jerome Foundation (a New York-based philanthropic organization that funds experimental art projects) could save him. In all, Spike spent $40,000 on it—much of it from his grandmother, who was to receive another producing credit—before he realized he was in over his head and retreated in shame. It didn't help that the powerful Screen Actors Guild refused to grant a waiver to include nonunion members in his cast. Had he been free of union grief, Spike might have finished *Messenger* after all.

It was a situation inexperienced filmmakers often find themselves in: that no matter how much they may have going for them, if the money falls through, everything shuts down. It is, therefore, no disgrace that this should have happened to Spike.

So Spike continued to work in various lowly positions in the film-business food chain, while continuing to live in a tiny basement apartment at 132 Adelphi Street, Fort Greene. It was in this humble, subterranean cubicle that 40 Acres and a Mule Filmworks was born—long before he moved to his present, prestigious headquarters at 124 Dekalb Avenue. Even so, this time was not wasted. Near his home, Spike would patronize a Myrtle Avenue pizzeria that would later inspire Sal's Famous in *Do the Right Thing*. He paid attention to the world around him and kept notes for potential film ideas in a journal. Most important, by living in Fort Greene Spike became friends with journalist Nelson George of the *Village Voice,* soon to become one of his strongest supporters in the press and an investor in *She's Gotta Have It*.

In those days, Spike had yet to adopt the B-boy uniform of Mars Blackmon and was still dressing in striped, button-down shirts with modest jackets and ties. His glasses were neither the square-framed Cazans of the *She's Gotta Have It* era nor the tasteful tortoise-shell rims he currently sports, but just the basic, conservative eyewear of the early eighties. And his hair was neither razor-cut nor even parted, but was merely kept in a modest, close-cropped

Eddie Murphy style an even half inch from his scalp all the way around. In short, he looked less a B-boy than a Buppie.

Spike claims never to have voted before 1984—not coincidentally the first time there was a serious challenge for the presidential candidacy by the Reverend Jesse Jackson. It seems incongruous that someone as politically astute—some would even say demagogic—as Spike couldn't be bothered to participate in the democratic process until he was twenty-seven. His politics, like those of most American Blacks, have remained staunchly Democratic ever since, his conversations peppered with unkind references to what he perceives the Reagan-Bush years as having done to America—especially black America.

In January of 1985, Spike got his first taste of publicity in a major publication. In a *Village Voice* roundup of up-and-coming young New Yorkers to watch for, journalist Carol Cooper wrote a brief item on Spike Lee. On the strength of *Joe's Bed-Stuy,* Cooper predicted that given the "financing he needs and deserves, screenwriter/director Spike Lee will make important contributions to the cinema of the '80s." The article correctly identified Spike not only as a "26-year-old Brooklyn native" but also as someone intent on bringing "intelligent stories about black American life to the screen using as much unexposed black talent as possible."

Even though the media was only just beginning to notice him, one fact was clear: where Spike Lee goes, controversy follows. There was already the hint that this five-foot-seven, 125 pound black Napoleon was going to make his mark on the world—even if no one could quite foresee to what an amazing extent. Only the most prescient would have guessed that this bespectacled bantamweight would soon be worshiped and detested in about equal measure the world over.

Although these were still the early days of the spotlight for Spike, the celebrity-in-training was already practicing his talent for agitation. Spike was quoted in the *Village Voice* as saying: "The best way to broaden media roles for black artists is for black people to get off their butts and start producing their own films. Blacks have enough collective clout moneywise to finance pictures, but we're still too busy investing in dry cleaners, liquor stores, and Cadillac dealerships. When we do start investing in movies, any profits should be put toward making more."

These are fine sentiments, and if Spike himself hasn't followed his own sensible strategies as religiously as he might, he's at least stayed closer to them than most. He does invest his own money in his own movies and encourages other high-profile members of the black bourgeoisie to do the same. And as he still drinks only reluctantly and still doesn't drive, there are no package stores or Cadillac dealerships on the horizon.

Chapter 3

1984–86: Just Do It

It is easier to be "African-American" than to organize oneself on one's own terms and around one's own aspirations and then, through sustained effort and difficult achievement, put one's insidious anti-self quietly to rest. No black identity, however beautifully conjured, will spare blacks this challenge that, despite its fairness or unfairness, is simply in the nature of things. But then I have faith that in time we will meet this challenge since this, too, is in the nature of things.

—SHELBY STEELE,
The Content of Our Character

Spike Lee began the year 1985 in a combination of depression and determination. His first feature had fallen through, yet he had to try again. He knew he couldn't let *The Messenger* be his one and only shot at the big time. Apart from not getting him where he wanted to be, the film had caused him to lose face with a lot of people who were important to him—not the least of whom was Grandma Zimmie Shelton.

But Spike is not the sort of man to stay down for long. Riffing on the 1956 Jayne Mansfield comedy *The Girl Can't Help It,* Spike entitled his script *She's Gotta Have It.* It was a provocative moniker that was guaranteed to get a reaction—either of admiration or dismay. Some of Spike's friends thought it sounded like it should be on the top shelf of the video store or perhaps in a plain brown wrapper. Some asked if Spike was abandoning serious filmmaking and going into pornography. But others knew a catchy phrase when they heard one and had the foresight to recognize that in those four words was the potential for a million-dollar smash.

On October 17, 1984, Spike wrote in his diary, "I can't see more than a two-week shoot, that's realistic. Small shoot, small payroll. Fuck it, I've learned my lesson this summer." He even added an emphatic, "NEVER AGAIN!" Moreover, he decided, he wanted to work with new, fresh individuals "who don't have the sour taste of last summer in their mouths." Monty Ross and Ernest Dickerson would be with him, of course, but otherwise he would find a new crew who wouldn't hold it against him that his previous project had not reached fruition. Spike compiled these thoughts, as well as his diary notes in *Spike Lee's Gotta Have It.*

Throughout the screenwriting process, Spike kept his vow not to talk about what he was up to with anyone not directly connected with the project, in the belief that those who do the most talking about moviemaking—like those who talk the most about sex—are the ones who are *doing* the least.

Spike cleverly combined the two. As he was writing *She's Gotta Have It,* he decided to do a little research so he could understand his female protagonist more deeply. He drew up a questionnaire with the help of his friend Mindy Goldman and had it filled out by thirty-five female friends—from virgins to Nola Darling-like "freaks"—asking for intimate details about their attitudes toward and experiences with sex. He got an amazingly strong response, considering the highly personal nature of the questions (such as, "Do you find a lot of men sexually inhibited?" "Can you enjoy sex without an orgasm?").

This novel form of research helped him make Nola Darling a more believable character. (Many women wish Spike had taken as much time and care with his female characters in his subsequent scripts.) Another thought that drove him to tackle this subject was the way males approach sex. "I have a lot of friends who like to talk about all the women they have," Spike pointed out to the *New York Times,* "but let a woman even think about having more than one man and they go berserk." It is this double standard that is at *SGHI's* intellectual center—and it was an enlightened and progressive move on Spike's part to want to wake up some of his fellows about their sexual hypocrisy. The film would be, he said, "a frank, open discussion of sex, something people have seen rarely in a film" (*Spike Lee's Gotta Have It,* p. 110).

For Spike, the script had to tell the truth not only about male-female relations, but also about race relations. It was always meant to be about something more than just the war between the sexes. "When

I wrote this script, I had a black audience in mind,"
Spike further noted in the book. "But that's not to
say that nobody else can enjoy it. It has been my
contention all along that an all-black film directed by
a black person can still be universal, just as has been
the case in the other arts. I mean, nobody stopped
coming to see Duke Ellington's music because he
had an all-black band."

To get these messages across, there were still
plenty of practical, hands-on, and even dreary things
to be done. On December 6, 1984, Spike had 40
Acres and a Mule incorporated at a cost of $450.
With its Afrocentric name (referring to a broken
promise made to slaves) and its deliberately unslick
logo, 40 Acres and a Mule defiantly announced itself
as an entertainment firm with a difference. It was
a sassy name to register with the government—
the act of a young kid with an attitude, but also
one with the talent to back it up. The militancy of
the corporation's name was somewhat softened by
Spike's jocular mottoes, also from black history and
culture: "By any means necessary," "Sho nuff," and
"Ya dig." And *She's Gotta Have It* would not be "a
Spike Lee film" but "a Spike Lee joint." Not content
just to play along, Spike had to reinvent the wheel.

Although his script was almost finished, Spike
was still writing longhand—and praying for a typewriter as his Christmas present. He was also fretting
about how the *Messenger* fiasco may have damaged
his reputation and credibility. Zimmie Shelton was
not worried about that, however: Spike's ever-
reliable grandmother staked him to $4,000 of her
own savings. He then had $14,000 with which to
make his dream project—not nearly enough, even

for a brilliant improviser, corner cutter, and fee deferrer like Spike. He simply had to have more.

Later that month, Spike worked on a pitch to do some writing for *The Cosby Show* with his film editor Barry Alexander Brown who, along with line producer John Kilik, is among Spike's closest white friends. The gag-writing gig didn't come through, which may be just as well: Spike didn't yet realize just how much *SGHI* was going to dominate his life over the next few months.

But, with shooting still half a year away, tempers were already rising: "Daddy and I can barely speak to each other without getting in an argument, but he's gonna do the music," he wrote in his diary. Spike spent the rest of the month "busting out" the script scene by scene and jotting notes about personal improvement, such as to "get rid of that slight speech impediment." (This "impediment" was nothing serious, only a slight stutter. In fact, Spike even found a way to turn it to his advantage when he created the immortal "Baby baby please baby please baby please please" routine for Mars Blackmon.)

Still, Spike was positively brimming over with ideas that winter of 1984–85, with diary entries like "I've got to go for broke" and "IDEA : We will shoot this film in beautiful black and white" and "Yo, we gotta get on it and stop fucking around, time is running out and we have to get with it" (p. 176). His urgency is palpable—yet expressed so many times throughout the book that his enthusiasm eventually grows tiresome.

Perhaps the last modest statement Spike Lee would ever make in his life was, "People will get tired of seeing Spike Lee in the credits, so

I'll just use my given name, Shelton Jackson Lee [for the producing credit]. Papa will be glad." (Actually, Spike ended up using "Shelton J. Lee" in the credits.) Spike has correctly identified the self-aggrandizing repetition of one name in credits as "the Sylvester Stallone syndrome"—which to Spike represented precisely the kind of showbiz crap he was determined to avoid.

"I'll say I'm a spiritual person, but not a very religious one," Spike told his diary (*Spike Lee's Gotta Have It*, p. 47). "I pray to my maker every night that on this project, *She's Gotta Have It,* things will work out right. Lord knows I don't need another heart-breaker like *Messenger*" (p. 117). Elsewhere, Spike writes that he planned some time in each day to "pray and meditate" (p. 201). He even uses the acronym GIMDAD, for "God is my defense and deliverance," a favorite phrase of Spike's. Exclamations like, "It was a desperate situation but the good Lord saw us through this one" and "I always want my work to have some spirituality about it" also crop up with a regularity that will surprise those who see Spike Lee only as a hard-headed ideologue.

Not that politics was unimportant to him even then. "I see messages there [in *SGHI*] but I rarely like to explain them or point them out," he wrote. This summation well explains why Spike Lee is such a good artist: although these heavy matters are impor-tant to him, he is not doctrinaire or narrow-minded about them. Not to care about them is the mark of a lightweight; to care about them exclusively soon makes an artist into a self-righteous bore.

But as 1985 dawned, Spike knew he had to forgo philosophy and get down to the serious business of raising capital. One of the first places Spike approached for some money was The Film Fund, a strongly feminist outfit which hesitated to underwrite a script they described as being so "sexist and problematic." Spike angrily retorted that his film would "not be sexist"—in fact, it would be "anything but." He assessed that the Film Fund's real objection was that "a MALE is doing a film like this." Had another feminist wanted to make a film about a woman with a healthy libido, it might have been a different story. But such are the peculiar politics of the arts-funding game.

It's a game with which he'd had a little experience the previous year. The American Film Institute (AFI), for instance, had given him $20,000 for *Messenger*. But Spike didn't understand that the grant was for that particular film. When he asked to apply the sum to *SGHI*, "those motherfuckers took the money back," Spike fumed.

Despite Spike's cries that this was racism in action, the Institute acted within its rights and was operating along its usual lines by refusing the transfer. As they approve grants not by filmmaker but by film, they would have done the same to anyone. But nobody could tell Spike this. He wrote the AFI a nasty letter of protest, hinting of bias and complaining for the first of many times, "We wuz robbed." (Here begins a string of incidents that have suggested to many of his critics that Spike is an extremely poor loser; that, no matter how petty, he can't simply accept defeat and then move on. But more about this later.)

Most of January and February were devoted to getting the money (or getting turned down) and rounding up the actors (or getting turned down). In March, Spike opened 40 Acres' first bank account—unfortunately, because his grants hadn't come through yet, he had no money to deposit. Like wishing for a typewriter for Christmas when just about every other screenwriter worked on computers, there is a simplicity and a poignancy about Spike's yearning, early days. Here was someone plainly bursting with talent, yet denied even the most basic resources to get his ideas out of his head and onto the screen.

He did, however, win on occasion. He was given $18,000 from the New York State Council on the Arts, with which he bought the film stock and shot *She's Gotta Have It*. Slowly, the necessary bucks did start trickling in, but it still wasn't enough, even for the barest of bare-bones productions.

By early June, investors were still not coming through for Spike the way he'd hoped they would. He ruefully mused in his diary, "If I don't do this film, I should at least get my driver's license this summer. Spike, it's time for you to learn how to drive." With or without a driver's license, Spike still needed $12,000—which, he knew, was "not gonna fall out of the sky." Even so, his mood remained one of confidence, not despair: "There was never the question, 'Will we get the money?' It was, 'We will get the money. We just don't know where it's at.'"

In June, Spike gave notice at First Run Features and, after three years there, he worked his last day. Spike had asked for a month off, yet both he and Seymour, his employer, must have known that it was over. They parted on good terms, with the understanding that Spike might want to come back some day. It was not to be, since the former film cleaner had a bigger job on the horizon: changing the course of cinema history.

The cast was coming together, even if the cash wasn't. Early readings of the script and rehearsals were going well, providing much-needed encouragement for 40 Acres during otherwise trying times.

Considering how little he could offer them for their services, Spike's search turned up a remarkable, young cast. His most important choice was his leading lady, and in actress Tracy Camilla Johns he found the perfect Nola Darling. "If you look at the media," Spike has said, "you'll see only one type of beautiful black woman: the classic octaroon-quadroon-mulatto-Vanity-Appollonia look. I thought this kind of thinking was restricted to America, but in my travels around the world, I've seen a lot of cultures trying to imitate the white American or European beauty standards." And, "I definitely wanted to attack that kind of mentality." With Johns, he found the alternative standard of beauty he was looking for.

(This is a theme that would continue throughout Spike Lee's films: that being black is something of which to be not ashamed, but *proud*. As he told the *New York Times*, "A lot of black artists start off with a black base, and once they get big, they get co-opted and cut all ties to the black community. That's when you start seeing the nose jobs and the jheri curls, the skin lightener and the music videos with the light-skinned love interests. What does it say when we see Michael Jackson changing his black African nose for a Caucasian nose? It's really sad, and I don't

think it is necessary to sell a record or do a movie."
She's Gotta Have It's closing credits even include
the instructive inscription, "This film was made with
no jheri curls and no drugs.")

For the men, Spike cast Tommy Hicks as the sensitive Jamie Overstreet and John Canada Terrell as the
insufferably vain male model Greer Childs. Looking
like a young Billy Dee Williams and dressing like a
GQ cover, Greer's beauty is truly skin deep. He con-
siders Brooklyn a lower-class borough and derides
Nola as "a typical Brooklyn tackhead"—something
she obviously is not. "I'm everything that you need,"
he boasts to her. Wrong again, pretty boy.

And then, of course, there was Mars, the hilarious
homeboy with the ten-speed mouth. "One of the reasons I put that character in was in direct response to
the Bernhard Goetz thing. Now, not every black kid
wearing a Kangol [hat] and hightop sneakers with fat
laces is going to rob you."

Spike has been so closely identified with the character of Mars Blackmon that it's hard to imagine
anyone else doing it. "I was halfway through writing
the script when realized I could play the part," Spike
wrote in *SLGHI*. "He is a combination of a lot of
people I know." So Spike, with no previous acting
experience beyond a grade school role of one of
the Seven Dwarfs, became a leading man in his
own film. Almost by accident he became not only
an instant *auteur* but also an instant movie star.

In order to look less Spike and more Mars, he had
his hair razor-cut in the latest style; otherwise, he just
slipped into character without any of the agonizing
or navel gazing about character and motivation that
gives actors a bad name. For one thing, Spike is a no-

nonsense kind of guy. For another, as writer, director and star, he simply had more pressing demands.

At this time, Spike had been dating a talented and attractive young dancer named Cheryl Burr. A diary notation from October 1984 reads, "I know I might be accused of being a Woody Allen but I'm seriously thinking of using my girlfriend Cheryl Burr somehow as a dancer in this." Following his logic that if a filmmaker has talented family and friends he'd be crazy not to milk them for all they're worth, Spike cast Burr as Ava, the dancer in the birthday sequence. Essentially a dancer rather than an actress, Spike gave her only one line (in bed, while Jamie is seeking relief from Nola with another woman) apart from her *pas de deux* by the monument. (Strangely, throughout *SLGHI* Spike seems to be on a first-name basis with everyone except his own girlfriend, whom he invariably refers to as "Cheryl Burr," or "my girlfriend Cheryl Burr," or even just "Burr"—long after it's been established who she is.) As for the Woody Allen reference, it's a comparison Spike was destined to get much of (and get tired of) once the movie came out.

On July 5, Spike began shooting. For mostly pragmatic reasons, he chose to start his filming at NYU. To keep things manageable, the first day's shooting was the simple but effective "Dog Scene." Set against a plain black backdrop, a string of African-American males—from the eminently desirable to the highly dubious—stare into the camera as they hit on Nola with a collection of come-on lines that must be heard to be disbelieved (for example, "You so fine, I drink a tub of your bathwater"). Spike chose to begin with it because it was simple and would start the shoot in a way that would make the cast and crew feel confident and upbeat. It remains one of the most fondly remembered scenes in the film.

Every day after shooting, Monty Ross would write begging letters and/or spend hours on the phone pleading with friends for hundreds, fifties, loose change, *anything*. Sometimes people would come through, sometimes they wouldn't. But, eventually, enough did that the film got finished.

By the 20th of July, after only eleven actual shooting days, it was a wrap. The fun was done, and the grueling labor of shaping raw footage into some kind of coherent statement was just beginning. Meanwhile, there was the equally grueling task of how to pay for it. But the point was that the twenty-eight-year-old Spike Lee had managed to do what he had been unable to accomplish the previous year: he had finished shooting a feature film. But, as many other young filmmakers in his position also discover, his troubles were far from over.

Originally Spike had wanted to shoot his break-through comedy the professional way, on 35 mm. color stock. But having learned the hard way about keeping his grasp within his reach, he was forced to settle for 16 mm. again, even though he was starting to feel constrained by its artistic and commercial limitations. (It's possible to take the cheaper 16 mm. format and blow it up to the 35 mm. that modern movie theaters require, though not without some loss of image sharpness. This has not stopped a number of films from recent years—including *Roger & Me* and *Straight Out of Brooklyn*—from achieving widespread acceptance and commercial success.)

He did finally settle on 16 mm. with a 35 mm.

blowup—and still got a fine-looking movie, thanks to Ernest Dickerson's talent with cameras and lighting. Only the color sequence in Fort Greene Park suffers from graininess. And Spike had grown to like the idea of shooting in black-and-white—especially when he saw how Dickerson could make his old neighborhood look with it.

This way, he brought the picture in for under $200,000. Spike's own best estimate of exactly how much the movie cost is $175,000 before advertising and promotion, only about $60,000 of which required actual cash. "It wasn't a matter of keeping costs to a certain level," he explains, but rather that it "was all the money we could get!" To comprehend the tiny miracle this really was, we must place these figures in their proper perspective. Consider that the average Hollywood picture these days costs $20 million—roughly 100 times as much!

Of course, choosing cheaper film stock was only part of it. Spike's austerity program also meant no unions, no completion bond, no insurance of any kind and no location permits from the Mayor's office. They had to shoot smash-and-grab style, with the crew moving in, getting their shots quickly, and getting out before any authority figures came along to ask for their permission slips.

In August, Spike was preparing to cut the film—while still trying to raise money to do it with. Even though *SGHI* was in the can, he had no money to rent editing facilities, mix the sound, score the music—or even to live on. The same problems he had confronted coming up with the cash to shoot he now faced again with editing costs. He also owed around $20,000 in back salaries to the many friends and acquaintances who had been kind enough to work for "deferments."

By September, he had the money situation sorted out enough that he could begin cutting. He also considered taking—then lost—a two-day-a-week audio-visual job at what he considered then to be a decent wage: $75 a day. Spike could certainly have used the cash at this point in his life, but in retrospect, it's probably best that he got by without it, allowing him to invest in himself.

Later that month, Spike and Pamm Jackson took a night off to see Martin Scorsese speak at an advance screening of his Griffin Dunne-Rosanna Arquette comedy *After Hours*. Afterward, Spike approached Scorsese to speak with him about the portrayal of Blacks in his films. Spike has always deeply admired Scorsese, and complimented the director on the "viciousness" of his high-powered camera movements and editing. Prior to the release of a single one of his films, though, Spike probably never thought it possible that in five years he would be using Scorsese's actors.

Such a prediction must have seemed like the flimsiest of fantasies to Spike in late 1985 when his entire movie was withheld by the lab for nonpayment of developing and printing bills—at one point, they even threatened to destroy it. Spike, miraculously, managed to keep a cool head throughout. "We'll get the money somehow" was his mantra.

By October, the ever-faithful Spike had rescued his print, completed cutting it, and was beginning to screen it for selected friends and potential investors. He knew he had a terrific selling point when in his book he described *SGHI* this way: "To be frank,

there's never been a black film like this, or maybe
a film in general." This was not boasting; it was
merely the truth. It is no exaggeration to say that
the innocent-looking reels sitting in Spike's humble
basement room were to change the face of black film
forever.

Even so, Spike missed his $200 November rent
payment and was also behind in his phone and Con
Edison bills for several hundred more. He'd also
been missing a few meals, his weight dropping to a
scant 115 pounds—dangerously low even for Spike
Lee. His "Mama" in Atlanta wired him $1,000—on
the understanding that it was not for the film but for
himself so that he wouldn't starve. Needless to say,
Spike spent a little on feeding himself, but mostly he
invested it in his dream.

The months of postproduction were exciting for
Spike, but also difficult financially: although he'd
made what appeared to be a wonderful film, Spike
first had to pay for its completion. All those hours in
the editing room would eventually bring him riches,
but in the meantime they only kept him in poverty,
as he was unable to hold a regular job and earn a
living. In December of 1985, Spike had written
in his journal with obvious agitation and urgency,
"Lately I've been meeting nothing but STIFF ART-
ISTS. A STIFF ARTIST is somebody who dangles
MONEY in front of my face only to SNATCH it
back at the last possible moment. They should be
shot" [emphasis in original]. A few days later, he
returned to the same theme: "From SOMEWHERE,
SOME ISLAND, I gotta get some money to finish
this GODDAMN movie" [emphasis in original]. As
though in direct answer to his blasphemous prayer,

Spike would get money from "some island": Island Pictures, the successful independent distributor.

What remained of 1985 was devoted to getting *SGHI* into a state fit for human consumption. Not only was his future riding on it, but so was his present: Spike felt he needed to see this one through to completion if only to clear his reputation after the previous year's aborted *Messenger*.

In January of 1986, after mixing the soundtrack with his father, Spike boasted that if Bill Lee's music "doesn't get nominated for an Academy Award for Best Original Score, they have tin drums for ears." This is the first of what would become a long-running series of Spike's demands for major awards. Then, as now, he was either unaware of or refused to acknowledge the reality that films made for under a million dollars aren't even considered by the millionaires' club called the Academy of Motion Picture Arts and Sciences to be worth mentioning. To get consideration, a film first has to be noticed. And Academy wisdom says that a film made for so little by people they've never heard of can't possibly be any good.

As it happened, awards were on the horizon—just not ones involving small gold-plated men with swords. When Spike took his pet project to the San Francisco Film Festival in April, the buzz began. A bidding war for the rights to distribute the film followed shortly.

The distributor who won the war was Island Pictures, a small but sensitive outfit that offered 40 Acres and a Mule a purse of $475,000—for something that had cost roughly one third of that amount. From Spike's standpoint, the picture had already

made a profit even before his royalties began. Spike
went with Island because he felt they had a good
record promoting "difficult" films—especially *Kiss
of the Spider Woman*. They also offered him a deal
for two more movies.

So *She's Gotta Have It* was bought and paid for
even before its public premiere at the Cannes Film
Festival on the French Riviera, the most famous
and prestigious film festival in the known universe.
The roaring reception at Cannes served to solidify
everyone's suspicions that *SGHI* was on its way to
being a very big hit. Although honored with a spot
in the Directors' Fortnight and the Prix de Jeunesse
(for outstanding newcomers), Spike really wanted
the *grand fromage,* the Camera d'Or. Usually, just
getting to Cannes is more than enough excitement
and ego-stroking for the first-time filmmaker. Not
Spike Lee, though: *he* had to have the top prize of
them all, and the French were a bunch of bigoted
Eurocentric mofos if they didn't give it to him! Even
back when he was a nobody, no amount of praise
could ever be enough to satisfy Spike's yelping need
for recognition and approval.

When Spike *does* take home an Oscar of his
own—and it's only a matter of time before he
does—his years of whining will only cause his
critics to complain that the Academy finally gave
in just to shut him up. The squeaky wheel may get
the grease, but it also breeds resentment.

Spike had been planning to take his creation
to the New York Film Festival, too, but once
the film was bought, there was no real need
anymore. Instead, he went straight into commercial release as soon as he could—August

1986—which was still a full year after it was shot. As it turned out, before the New York Film Festival could have shown it in late September, *SGHI* had already made millions of dollars.

But this was not before it had cleared one last hurdle: getting the Motion Picture Association of America's (MPAA) Classification and Ratings Administration (CARA) to approve it for American screens. At first, the MPAA found the sex scenes too explicit for the "Restricted" (no one under 17 admitted without adult accompaniment) rating that Island Pictures had insisted upon in their contract. Instead, they wanted to give *She's Gotta Have It* the dreaded "X" for being, in the MPAA's quaint, schoolmarmish parlance, "saturated with sex."

The "X" (now renamed the somewhat less damning NC-17, or No Children Under 17, regardless of adult accompaniment) was considered box office poison in America; many theater chains across the country had a policy against booking them. Spike would cut and recut his film no less than three times before the MPAA backed down and gave him the "R" rating he so desperately needed. As much as Spike, like most filmmakers, wanted to preserve his original vision, no "R" rating meant no release. He therefore had no choice but to try trimming the offending scenes as little as possible before resubmitting the film to try again. Eventually, Spike did make *SGHI* meet MPAA standards for non-pornographic mainstream entertainment, but he wasn't happy about it.

Spike's tart assessment of the situation in his book was that "The MPAA, like Hollywood itself, has trouble relating to black sexuality. I don't think

it's out-and-out racist, but the film portrays blacks
outside stereotypical roles," Spike said at the time
because "when it comes to black sexuality, they
don't know how to deal with it. They feel uncomfortable. There are films with more gratuitous sex
and even violence [than *SGHI*]. *Nine and a Half
Weeks* got an 'R.' And look at *Body Double*."

There's no denying the man has a point here.
At the time, Spike expressed hope that his own
unrated "director's cut" of the film could later be
released on home video. The problems associated
with circulating two different cassettes of the same
movie proved too cumbersome, and the standard-
issue North American version prevailed. He did,
however, promise to get the film in all its unabridged
glory released in Europe. (This, unfortunately, still
has yet to happen: for the sake of simplicity, the
standard, eighty four-minute U.S. version was issued
worldwide.)

After all, pornographic films don't usually begin
with literary quotations. Despite being one of the fun-
niest comedies of its year, *She's Gotta Have It* begins
on a deceptively somber note:

> Ships at a distance have every man's wish on
> board. For some they come in with the tide.
> For others they sail forever on the horizon,
> never out of sight, never landing until the
> Watcher turns his eyes away in resignation,
> his dreams mocked to death by Time. That is
> the life of men.
> Now, women forget all those things they don't
> want to remember, and remember everything
> they don't want to forget. The dream is the

truth. Then they act and do things accordingly.

The quotation is from Harlem Renaissance writer Zora Neale Hurston's *Their Eyes Were Watching God*. Spike tried to get a photo of Hurston to use in his opening credits, but had to settle for just running her words in white lettering on a black screen. He'd also considered filming Monty Ross reading this passage. Most viewers would agree he made the right decision to run it the way he did.

But then, when a movie succeeds both critically and commercially to the satisfying extent that *She's Gotta Have It* has, clearly its creators were doing *something* right. "Black filmmakers have been locked into a Hollywood mentality," Spike concluded in the *Village Voice*. "They think it takes millions of dollars to make a film, so they spend years going around to the studios begging for money. For me, the most important thing about this movie— aside from whether or not people like it—is that it be shown as an example of a young black filmmaker who, without half the means of a Hollywood director, made his movie," he stressed. "It can be done."

It *was* done. And Spike Lee's life would never be the same.

Chapter 4

1986: *She's Gotta Have It*

"I knew it would be a hit," said Spike, as *She's Gotta Have It's* takings crossed the $5 million mark. "But I thought it might take a little longer."

When *She's Gotta Have It* opened in the fall of 1986, writer-director-star Spike Lee was just a sassy kid from Brooklyn with a camera and an arts grant. He'd shot his debut on 16 mm., black-and-white stock for a price that wouldn't keep Steven Spielberg in turtlenecks. Lee's cast were not only unknowns, but several had never acted before. Across the country, the picture played to a true rainbow coalition of audiences. Spike got his message through to his constituency—and several others besides—for a variety of reasons, including good press, adroit promotion, sexy subject matter, astute timing and more than a little luck.

Shortly before its August 16, 1986, opening night, the Black Filmmaker Foundation hosted a premiere for *She's Gotta Have It*. That his proud, robust expression of the contemporary black scene received an enthusiastic reception among his peers was no surprise to Spike.

But then, neither was the film's subsequent success when it first opened commercially. Spike just took everything in stride, as though he'd been expecting it all along. During the first week that it was playing to a paying public (at the now-closed Cinema Studio on Broadway around 68th Street), Spike practically made his home outside the theater. There on the sidewalks of Manhattan's predominantly liberal-Jewish Upper West Side, Spike would hang around under the marquee trying to flag down passersby on Broadway to come in and see his movie. He handed out buttons advertising the film to those waiting in line at showtime and even peddled *She's Gotta Have It* T-shirts and soundtrack albums in the lobby.

After two weeks, the *SGHI* juggernaut had gathered enough momentum to open at more theaters—adding venues until *SGHI* at one point was playing on eighteen screens in the New York area and 150 coast to coast. Spike's little $175,000, eleven-day wonder wound up pulling in an astonishing $8.5 million. After that, even, it went on to a long and healthy life on video.

On the hot August night of the premiere, Spike and company took themselves downtown from the Upper West Side to SoHo and threw themselves a release celebration at the Puck Building, a popular party venue in an historic Manhattan setting. There Spike remained composed and reserved even in the face of the embarrassingly gushing praise and adulation. In his colossally oversized *She's Gotta*

Have It T-shirt—more of a smock, really—he stayed cool both emotionally and physically. Among the onslaught of compliments, people also told Spike (repeatedly) that they knew women like Nola— "which I find amusing," he told *Women's Wear Daily*. "I had to make her up for the movie because I've never known anyone like her at all."

Before the year was out, Spike would even make his first appearance on a *Saturday Night Live* broadcast hosted by *The Cosby Show*'s Malcolm Jamal-Warner, with musical guests Run-DMC, a rap group of whom the director remains fond. With all this happening for him, Spike should have been one happy man, and for the most part, he was.

But he knew that this wasn't enough. The tremendous sense of urgency that had troubled him since Morehouse drove him to speak out at every opportunity and to make the most of what he thought might be his only chance to be heard. At the time, Spike— and everybody else—still thought he might be just a fluke, a one-hit wonder, given his Warholian fifteen minutes in the spotlight, then forever returned to the shadows. And, had Spike not been such a persistent individual, that might well have been the case.

One of the things troubling him in 1986—and which still troubles him today—was what he perceived as insufficient recognition for his work. In October of that year he told *Film Comment* magazine: "We was [sic] robbed of the Camera d'Or" [the top Cannes prize in the newcomers' category]. Such complaints about honors denied him—usually directed at the Academy Awards, though occasionally at Cannes juries—have become an obsession of his.

This is in stark contrast to the Introduction page of *Spike Lee's Gotta Have It*: "It's not for me to say whether *SGHI* is a landmark film (I make 'em, that's all)."

To most people, this does not sound like an accurate representation of the way Spike's mind works. There *are* filmmakers out there who genuinely care only about their work, and not the reaction to it. Spike Lee, however, isn't one of them.

Within weeks of his first commercial movie's release, Spike Lee was already establishing a reputation among Blacks for this kind of straight talk and plain dealing. Love it or hate it, there's no mistaking where Spike Lee stands when he starts to open his mouth. His contemporaries immediately recognized that this was not just another grinning "Knee-grow" (Malcolm X's disdainful term for Uncle Toms) willing to sing and dance for his supper. This one was not going to be just another faithful servant of the white entertainment empire, content to shut his mouth and count his cash. People said that Spike was one crossover who wouldn't sell out, ignore his roots, or turn his back on his old friends. And they were (mostly) right.

Technically, the film itself was, while not crude, somewhat marginal. His jump-cuts, particularly of Greer and Nola in bed, were awkward and screamed Film School. He suffered the jerkiness of a hand-held camera where the smoothness of a Steadicam would have been better. He used a montage of stills to convey a subway ride when there was no particular reason to—except of course the overriding reason that filming on the subway is more expensive than having your photographer brother snap a few stills. Similarly, he used a traditional-sounding jazz soundtrack rather than something more contemporary like hip-hop less because of artistic rationale than because of his father.

These things can all be forgiven of the struggling "guerrilla filmmaker." But there's a certain lack of sophistication in the writing, too, and that's less forgivable. The joke of Greer's meticulous undressing and folding of his clothes is dragged on long after everyone's gotten the point that the man is vain. As Mars, Spike gets off some genuinely funny lines, but Tommy Hicks's Jamie is stuck playing straight man to the buffoons on either side of him. As for Nola, she is definitely an original creation, but what do we really learn about her other than her love of sex?

It's surprising to go back to *She's Gotta Have It* now if you haven't seen it since it first came out. Although it is still a charming little film, Spike's recent work makes *little* the operative word. There are good scenes, but also a few awkward ones. Spike himself shows less maturity as an actor than he now has—which should not be surprising since he trained only in directing, not performing. In fact, all the actors occasionally come across as stiff and unconvincing, something even Spike has noticed. He finds the film hard to watch today, blaming his own inexperience for not knowing enough about how to direct actors, how to tell them what they need to hear.

The birthday sequence, depending on the viewer's mood, is either a delightful diversion or, in the words of one critic, "enough to make [*An American in Paris* director] Vincent Minnelli turn in his grave." The quality of the color photography, though adequate, makes one glad to return to black-and-white (which blows up to 35 mm. much more successfully).

And although it doesn't address the complexion issue like *School Daze*, the film does investigate class distinctions within black society: whereas Greer drives a Jaguar convertible, Mars rides a ten-speed. Greer proposes a toast "to our careers"; Mars shoots back, "What careers? I haven't had a job in two years." Mars claims not only to have met the Reverend Jesse Jackson, but to have been the first to put the idea into the Reverend's head that he should seek office: "Run, Jesse, run!" Greer dismisses Mars and Jamie as "ignorant ghetto Negroes."

Mars really gets it from Greer—and the audience sides with the former against the latter, just as Spike intended them to do. "B-boys have a really bad reputation," the director has said, "and I wanted to show that they weren't all criminals and drug addicts." Right from the start, Spike set out to overturn Hollywood stereotypes of black people; it's a crusade he has pursued throughout his career.

Spike has often cited *Rashomon*, the 1951 classic by the brilliant Japanese director Akira Kurosawa, as one of his influences for making *SGHI*. In *Rashomon*, a rape-murder is reported by four different people (including a ghost) in four very different ways. Each has his or her version of what happened, each of which sounds convincing yet contradicts the others. Hence, we are treated not only to the opinions of Nola's trio of eligible bachelors, but also those of her roommate (Joie Lee), her lesbian friend Opal (Raye Dowell), her father (Bill Lee) and even sex therapist Dr. Jamison (Epatha Merkinson). Unlike *Rashomon*, however, there is little disagreement among the interpretations.

From Warren Beatty's *Reds* (1981), Spike admits to borrowing the idea of "witnesses" against black backdrops—the parade of "dogs," for instance—speaking directly into the lens. He's also mentioned drawing inspiration from Francis Ford Coppola's *The Outsiders* (1983), Jean-Luc Godard's *Breathless* (1959), *The Wizard of Oz* (1939), and even classic Hollywood musicals *Singin' in the Rain* (1952) and *An American in Paris* (1951).

There's no denying *SGHI* is awkward in parts or that Spike tries a couple of things that just don't come off. But all in all, it's an impressive debut—funny, charming, realistic and refreshingly honest about both race and sex—and one that would have brought notice to a young director in any country and with any complexion.

Island Pictures billed *She's Gotta Have It* with the irresistible slogan, "A seriously sexy comedy"—a brilliant strategy, as it turned out. The film *is* very sexual, but also very sensual. It's not at all pornographic, but tastefully done.

She's Gotta Have It struck a chord with mid-eighties moviegoers. Yet it was an extremely unusual mainstream release in many ways. That so many people went to see what is essentially an ambitious student film is slightly amazing. What were the circumstances that made it a hit with the black community, and how did their reaction spur white audiences to give it a chance?

More interesting than its cinematic merits and flaws, what makes *SGHI* fascinating is its acceptance in the marketplace. A picture can never make the serious money until it plays the suburbs. A small "art" film can do respectable business in one or two major markets (*Paris Is Burning, Prospero's Books*), even though it may take months. But grosses don't get into the millions until the film is shown in the rest of the country (*Europa, Europa, La Cage aux Folles*). *She's Gotta Have It* was marketed to primarily urban (black) audiences, first to full houses in New York and later invading Trenton, Philadelphia, Boston and points beyond.

In the years preceding *SGHI*, there had been a dearth of films for the black market. Blaxploitation heroes had been put out to pasture. Other than the odd prestige project like the excellent *A Soldier's Story* and the problematic *The Color Purple* that somehow managed to creep through the cracks, Hollywood seemed to have joined the Reagan Revolution in shifting black issues to the back burner. A sizable portion of the American population was being either ignored or stigmatized as crime-prone welfare cheats.

In a mere eighty-four minutes, Spike Lee and *SGHI* effectively challenged the status quo of the entire decade with a film containing something for almost everyone in the black community. It demonstrated a simple fact that eight decades of American moviemakers hadn't grasped: that there were all kinds of black folks, not just the demonic stereotype that had been subtly encouraged back into fashion. There were Blacks who were intelligent, who were independent, who were sincere, insincere, hard-working, witty, silly, vain, etc.

Looking back from our present, post-Spike perspective, it's hard to believe it was ever considered news that black society contained millions of very different individuals who fall in love, have dreams, and struggle to find their own brand of happiness. At a time when Blacks had little in the way of a positive public image with which to identify (other than Jesse Jackson and the usual elite of athletes and singers), this was nothing short of liberating. When had moviegoers ever had the chance to experience a character like Nola Darling? A film as frank about women as this one is rare no matter what race the character. That Nola was black—and provided a screen presence for black women that had never been granted them before outside of fantasy figures like Coffy or Cleopatra Jones—makes her nothing less than a cinema landmark.

"Even the top stars like Eddie Murphy and Richard Pryor never get to have any love interest in their films," Spike has complained to *Women's Wear Daily*, asking rhetorically, "How often have you seen a black man and woman kiss on the screen?" Or, for that matter, when was the last time anyone saw movie Blacks playing Scrabble? (Typically, though, Spike uses the game to raise the question of whether black English—in this case, "gonna"—is "a real word." Clearly, Spike was gonna have his say throughout *Gotta*.)

Blacks started to flock to the film for several reasons. First, it was a sympathetic look at themselves when there were no others like it around. Second, it had a lot of sex (or so the rumor was), which itself guaranteed a certain customer base. Third, it was *funny*—and even those who didn't care about its subtler messages could still enjoy it on a superficial level. Lastly, it was provocative for audiences who do require a little more in the way of intelligence. Blacks began turning out in large numbers.

And once they did, *SGHI* started getting noticed by the white audiences, who saw that something was going on but couldn't quite figure out what it was. Soon, the film was not just a black thing but a crossover sensation. Whites could satisfy their curiosity about the black experience vicariously, or just show their solidarity with the black community in the face of Reaganism. How much of this was genuine and how much was posing is debatable, but it was nonetheless unusual and refreshing to see mainstream audiences at a black flick with no guns, coke, kung fu or hip-hop.

Speaking of solidarity, Spike had originally intended to make Greer a West Indian immigrant "fronting" as an African-American, as further proof of the character's shallowness and phoniness. That Spike would use someone's nationality as a way of discrediting his character is deeply disturbing and perpetuates the same tired, West-Indians-come-here-and-think-they're-better-than-us noise that guaranteed that America's biggest audience for reggae and calypso would be white people. The idea that being from another country makes you less desirable as a person—another black person, remember—is not only deeply offensive, but also the kind of "disunity" among Blacks of which Spike would soon be complaining in *School Daze*. It is also the sort of racial insult that would have Spike screaming bloody murder were it applied to American Blacks. (At least Spike had the sense to dump Nola's didactic and sickeningly "uplifting" final soliloquy in which she vows she "will never forsake the Black man"—one of those ideas the filmmaker gets now and then that are better left on the drawing board.)

These arguments aside, *She's Gotta Have It* stands out as one of Spike Lee's most fondly remembered and least controversial works. "The whole point," he told the *New York Times* that November, "is that you can take an unknown, all-black cast and put them in a story that comes from black experience, and all kinds of people will come to see it if it's a good film. I wish Hollywood would get that message."

Interviewed by Edmund Newton in the *Daily News Magazine* the previous August, Spike complained (as he would on many, many other occasions) about white screenwriters' reluctance to deal with black romance or sexuality. Commented Newton, "You get the feeling that things may be a little different now that Spike Lee is on the scene." A prescient pronouncement, though Newton probably had no way of knowing just how different.

During the arduous eighteen months Spike spent writing, prepping, making and editing *SGHI*, he kept notes. With typical cockiness, he had tried to sell them to a publisher as a "Making of" book even before he had sold the movie itself. Unsurprisingly, no publisher was interested in taking on a volume about a film that might not even get distribution. After it did get distribution—and especially after its very wide distribution—a publisher did come through, and Spike's publishing career was born a few months after his movie career had been. More than just anecdotes from the set, Spike carefully laid out for the aspiring independent filmmaker exactly what it takes to work guerrilla style. Three similar books followed his next three movies, though none captured the raw excitement of overcoming the odds and defying convention in a mad effort to get a vision out of the typewriter and onto a projector.

Because by this time, the man who'd just gotta have it, had got it. Now he had to figure out how to keep it.

Chapter 5

1987–88:
Big Man On Campus

After the success of *She's Gotta Have It*, both
Spike Lee and Island Pictures were happy to sign
a two-picture deal together. But it soon became
apparent that the kind of large-scale musical that
Spike wanted to make was just out of Island's
financial range.

As much as Spike complained about Island's
reluctance to give him the money he needed, he
couldn't seem to understand that Island is only a
small, moderately successful company outside the
mainstream of the industry and simply didn't have
that kind of money to throw around. Yes, Spike *did*
need more than the $4 million ceiling Island was
putting on his production. But his contention that
Island was cramping his style was misguided.

The truth was, it was time for Spike to move
on. For the kind of movies he wanted to make, he

needed the backing of a major studio. So the night Island president Russell Schwartz had his assistant wake Spike up at home to tell him they were bailing out of *School Daze* was a blessing in disguise. Although he would now have to "go shopping" with his script, at least he wouldn't face the trimming of musical numbers and general scaling down of his vision that Island would have required.

Island had also had concerns that the subplot about apartheid and divestiture would make *School Daze* seem dated very quickly, that it was the kind of topical, momentary reference which would not withstand the scrutiny of time. They felt that if Spike were serious about being a filmmaker for the ages and not just for the moment, he should try to avoid such temporal touches that sparkle briefly, then quickly lose their appeal. And there *is* something to be said for avoiding the strictly timely issues of the day: like political satire, nothing is more pertinent when fresh and nothing more boring when stale.

Although it came second, *School Daze* is, in a way, the earliest of all the Spike Lee joints. He had written a script for a black college comedy—tentatively titled *Homecoming*—even before he wrote *She's Gotta Have It*. Because of the costs and complications of mounting such a large-scale project, Spike wisely opted to start small, launching his professional moviemaking career with the more manageable *SGHI*.

Having mastered the barest of bare-bones productions—and having exceeded all expectations—Spike felt ready to move on to bigger (if not better) things. This time, his budget would be about thirty

times that of *SGHI*. This time, he had longer to
rehearse than he had had for the entire shooting
of his first film: two weeks' rehearsal, followed by
eight weeks' shooting. This time, he'd be working
in color, and in 35 mm. He'd have professional
actors and a professional crew. This time, he'd
really show them what he could do.

So why is *School Daze* generally regarded as
Spike's least satisfying effort? As innumerable
big-budget Hollywood disasters from *Cleopatra* to
Heaven's Gate will attest, money can't buy good
judgment.

Like *Homecoming* before it, *School Daze* was to
take place on the campus of a black college, but the
political angle to the story was fundamentally different. The issue in *Homecoming* had been a black
college's potential absorption into the state system;
in *School Daze*, it was the institution's implication
in apartheid through its holdings in South African
corporations. But if he wanted his audience to think
about politics, he'd first have to seduce them with
parties, sex and the "hazing" of fraternity induction
rituals. Then, when their defenses were down, he'd
hit them with his real purpose: to tell Blacks to
wake up and realize that there is more to life than
selfish pleasure seeking. That, in fact, the race faced
challenges not just from the Man, but from each
other. That the petty differences between them—
particularly over lightness of skin and straightness
of hair—had consequences which were seriously
impairing solidarity and advancement.

These frictions, largely unknown outside the
black community, date back to slave days, when
lighter-skinned "house Negroes" were given the

preferred jobs inside the mansion while the darker-complected "field Negroes" were stuck with the backbreaking stoop-labor of picking cotton in the blazing sun. It was a caste system both created and enforced by Whites, yet today most Whites are unaware of its existence. Spike's determination to go public with the petty but persistent jealousies between light- and dark-skinned Blacks was decried as "washing our dirty laundry in public" by some of the more conservative black leaders.

These are touchy topics, difficult to dramatize in a popular entertainment—especially one consisting largely of blindfolded fraternity "pledges" being forced to eat dog food and stick their hands down toilets.

A problematic film to produce, *School Daze* remains equally problematic film to watch. Film-making ought to get easier with practice but, from the casting onward, Spike faced obstacles and unexpected setbacks with *Daze*. He was taking on a project roughly twenty-five times the size of *She's Gotta* and felt the need for it to be twenty-five times as good. Other than having to shut down the whole deal as he'd done with *Messenger*, it was the most stressful experience of Spike's young life. He has succinctly described the forty-nine-day shoot as "frustrating as shit." Many viewers feel that way about the results. The combining of comedy and message was certainly ambitious, but, both prac-tically and aesthetically, Spike was simply taking on more than he could handle.

Although Spike had more money to play with on his second time out, he also had more on which to spend it. In its own way, *Daze* was just as much of an economic ordeal as *She's Gotta Have It*. Because of the shoot's very real financial limitations—*you* try mounting a two-hour musical comedy on location for under $6 million—there were setbacks involving personnel.

Veteran actors like Ossie Davis and Joe Seneca worked for less than they were worth just to be part of what they considered an important chapter in black film history (and to establish a fruitful relationship with an up-and-coming director). Typically, it was the younger, less experienced actors who gave the headaches to Spike and casting director Robi Reed.

Early in 1987, Spike's girlfriend Cheryl Burr took over from Erica Gimpel as one-quarter of the sorority singing group, the Gamma Rays, after Gimpel began to wonder aloud if her role was large enough. Gimpel wanted to think about it some more. Spike told her to get in or get out. She got out.

Despite her close relationship with the director, Burr didn't end up playing the part either. Early in rehearsals, she broke a bone in her foot. The part of the fourth Gamma Ray finally went to Frances Morgan, the production's assistant choreographer.

Vanessa Williams, the temporary Miss America who was crowned, then denied, the title in a nude-photo scandal in 1985, had been Spike's original choice for the role of Jane. Because of Williams's fame, she would have marquee value. But casting director Robi Reed finally convinced Spike that Tisha Campbell was preferable for two reasons: not only could she sing well, but, at eighteen, she had an innocence and sweetness that the part seemed to require. When Jane gets dumped by the heartless Julian, the audience feels for her in a way they might not have done for someone as self-confident as Vanessa Williams.

But worse struggles still lay ahead, not with casting but with location. Spike had wanted to shoot at his beloved alma mater, Morehouse College at the Atlanta University Center. As a third-generation Morehouse grad, Spike obviously had a strong attachment to the place. The following spring, Spike began shooting on the Morehouse campus, though still no contract had been signed. The university wanted to see Spike's shooting script—a common enough request from any host location. Spike resolutely refused, knowing they would not be pleased with the girl chasing, game playing, defying of authority and laundry airing running through its various plot fragments.

The college objected on the grounds that Spike was not planning to present a "positive" image of life at the contemporary black campus; that it dwelt on the rowdy and the lusty—not to mention the divisive and the contentious. The first shooting Spike had done at Atlanta University, where the crew had hung banners calling for divestment of all South African holdings, had tipped the other colleges off to potential controversy. So did the rowdiness of the audience during rehearsals for the fraternities' "Greek Show" at the homecoming party. The height of absurdity was reached when one faculty member even objected to actor Joe Seneca's looks, claiming this dignified, white-haired gentleman should not be cast as a college president because he looked like "a plantation man"! And the school's serious-minded deans and professors could not have been impressed by the fact that Spike's film would contain not one scene set in a classroom: Spike didn't just undervalue the learning aspect of college life, he avoided it altogether. Even the otherwise brain-dead *Animal House* included a professor among its characters (albeit one who smoked dope with his students).

The reputation of Spike's previous movie wasn't helping his case, either. *She's Gotta Have It* had yet to open in the South, and word had got round that it was pornographic—not an unreasonable assumption on the basis of the title. Still, they should have based their arguments on evidence, not hearsay.

So with his scheduled first day of shooting fast approaching, Spike felt he had no choice but to begin, with or without permission. After all, the guerrilla-style smash-and-grab had served him well enough on *She's Gotta Have It*.

Principal photography commenced March 8, 1987, as Atlanta was warming up for spring. A suitably moving and profound send-off was provided by the Reverend Jesse Jackson, who gave cast and crew his blessings. Aware of what this young filmmaker and his disciples were going through, the Rev. Jackson prayed for *School Daze*'s safe and speedy completion. The production then moved to New York for the dance scenes (where the best dancers are), shooting on a soundstage in Brooklyn (where, according to Spike Lee, the best of everything is).

As for Spike's directorial style, star Larry Fishburne has described it as loose and improvisatory. Having worked under control freaks like Francis Ford Coppola (in *Gardens of Stone*),

Fishburne found Spike's modus operandi offered almost too much freedom. Despite having wanted more specific direction from Spike, Fishburne still managed to turn in a fine performance and was singled out by many critics for being better than the film he was in.

Actors recall being permitted a lot of room to ad lib. In fact, they had to, as Spike's script was, according to one, "not much more than a blueprint." Spike wanted the conversation to sound unforced, even improvised. In a classic case of don't-try-this-at-home-kids, Spike's strategy for achieving natural dialogue was not to write enough of it. Fishburne's monologue about how Blacks would get on any bus offering free beer and chicken, for instance, was of his own devising.

But after three weeks of work, the college administration delivered an ultimatum that simply couldn't be ignored. In the words of a Morehouse football chant, Spike and company had to "Take your hat, your coat, and *leave*, motherfucker!" Not only could Spike not shoot at the college any more, he would not even be permitted to use the many thousands of feet of film he'd already shot. One can sympathize somewhat with the administration's decision. Negro colleges, always scraping to make ends meet and keep their doors open, are embattled enough just trying to pay the rent without Northern trouble-makers showing up to complicate things. They also feel that, as they have trouble getting the white academic establishment to take them seriously in the first place, they must be vigilant about maintaining an air of dignity and discipline. These were goals that *Daze* did not seem to advance.

So *School Daze* faced one of the worst things that can happen to a movie once shooting has commenced: it lost its location. And the blow to the production was more than merely logistical; coming from a proud tradition of Morehouse men, Spike was genuinely hurt by the snub.

Spike and company had planned to hold a benefit screening of *She's Gotta Have It* in Atlanta. As the movie had not yet played in Georgia, Spike was arranging a fancy fund-raising premiere, complete with cast. By charging $15 a ticket, they could net $6,000 for the college in one evening. But because of *She's Gotta*'s racy reputation, the school's elders nixed that one, too.

These events were, ironically, a real-life enactment of exactly the kind of disagreements among Blacks that Spike's script was trying to investigate. But any such reflections about how his fiction was coming true all around him would have to wait: for the moment, he just needed a place to set up his cameras and lights.

The filmmaker stood firm on his artistic choices. He was going to tell his black-college story *his* way or not at all. He and the older generation had a fundamental difference of opinion on what constitutes the best for their people, with each side accusing the other of holding back the race. In his next book *Uplift the Race: The Construction of "School Daze"* Spike stated his case. "I refuse to be caught in the 'negative image' trap that's set for black artists. Yes, black people have been dogged in the media since Day One [but] we overreact when we think that every image of us has to be 100 percent angelic [and] Christ-like."

A parallel can be found in the way many young Blacks feel about the "perfect Negro" movies Sidney Poitier made in the 1960s: that Poitier's wholesome image may have been what was needed at the time, but that time has passed. Despite their unequivocal admiration for the barriers broken by Poitier and for the superb quality of his best work, the current thinking is that to perpetuate this image would be counterproductive.

The nerves that Spike struck on campus also reverberated off campus and through the wider community. Many black statesmen, particularly those of the old school, were of the opinion that they had enough trouble and they resented the divisions Spike ignited in the community. These arguments whined on through the summer and fall of 1987 as Spike assembled his film.

At 9:00 A.M. on Christmas morning, Spike sat down and wrote some notes about what he wanted to do with his next film. He already had a title for it: *Do the Right Thing*.

Five days later, Spike made another diary entry, this time regarding Bill Lee: "My father will compose the score for the film [*Do the Right Thing*]. We have our problems, but they are always overcome." Reading these words, few could know the true nature of the conflicts between Spike and Bill Lee. The official story was artistic differences. The straight dope was something else: a concerned son's disapproval of his father's explorations in an artificial paradise of heroin. Privately, Spike worried about his father's condition; publicly, he couldn't mention it.

Realizing that he was on a roll, Spike was already

thinking well ahead into the future: "After *Do the Right Thing*, I might do *The Autobiography of Malcolm X*. The project is at Warner Brothers, and Denzel Washington, who played Malcolm in an off-Broadway play, is interested in the film role."

"I've been blessed with the opportunity to express the views of black people who otherwise don't have access to power and the media," Spike has said after shooting *School Daze*. "I have to take advantage of that *while I'm still bankable*" [emphasis added].

Running through both Spike's work and his life is the idea that time is running out, that his acceptance is a temporary fluke and will vanish as unexpectedly as it arrived. It's an obsession that parallels Malcolm X's impatience with anyone who didn't wear a watch—and also Public Enemy's habit of wearing clocks around their necks to indicate they "know what time it is." It's an urgency Spike has yet to lose—and which helps to charge his films with the electric energy that makes them such compelling viewing.

Unfortunately for Spike, during the time he was making *School Daze*, there was a changing of the guard at Columbia Pictures, the company that had taken over financing from Island. David Puttnam, the strong-willed, quality-minded Englishman whom Columbia's board of directors had imported to straighten out the troubled studio and who had supported *School Daze* to the fullest, was let go. So was his Spike-positive collaborator, David Picker. In their place was installed Dawn Steel, a tough executive as famous for getting results as for alienating the artists in her stable.

One such alienated artist was Spike Lee, who

dubbed the new CEO "Steely Dawn." (Spike may or may not have coined the name, but he certainly helped to popularize it, brandishing it like a weapon at every interview opportunity.) Steel, Spike felt, did not understand what he was trying to do with *School Daze* and may even have been hostile to the whole project.

As with the aborted benefit screening, Spike had originally planned to hold a coming-out party for *School Daze* on behalf of the Morehouse. But by this point, too much hostility had been engendered on both sides to make such an event anything worth celebrating. "We were going to do a premiere in Atlanta. Now we'll do it in New York," Spike reported. "We need a warm reception, and there are too many people, powerful people, in Atlanta who wish we'd never come."

So back he went to New York. But no warm reception awaited.

Chapter 6

Dazed and Confused

*One thing the white man never can give the
black man is self-respect!*
—The Autobiography of Malcolm X

In January of 1988, Spike was very agitated about
the upcoming release of *School Daze*. Columbia
wanted to delay it until March, because Lorimar was
putting a lot of marketing muscle behind their Carl
Weathers-Vanity shootemup, *Action Jackson*. Spike
was upset that Columbia saw black people as "one
monolithic audience" with no variety in their tastes.
Or, it was implied, who weren't mentally equipped
to deal with more than one movie at a time. Either
way, Spike felt Hollywood was giving its black customers the big dis.

Come February, Spike's fury with Columbia for
not supporting *Daze* was growing. He threatened
that if the studio did not get behind the picture

substantially more than it had so far done—particularly in *Ebony, Jet*, and *Emerge* and other black media—he and his comrades would put up the subway posters themselves if they had to. The executives thought Spike was bluffing. He called them on it. Perhaps more for his own publicity than the film's, the most acclaimed young black movie director in the country and a few of his friends got out buckets of paste and did just that.

But then, nothing about *School Daze* is traditional. The source of most of the drama (and even much of the comedy) is the conflict between fair-skinned and dark-skinned students at a fictional black institution tellingly named Mission College. Works involving color almost always pit one race against another. Movies and stories derived from intragroup conflicts based on *shades* of the same color are rare.

Its stated theme may be black disunity, but *School Daze* also addresses lack of black self-respect—a problem often at the root of other, more obvious problems. After 400 years, Blacks are finally getting a little respect and are beginning to get their due in the white world. But *self*-respect is a different matter; not something from outside, but from within. These are serious concerns for what appears on the surface to be little more than a hastily pasted-together collection of low-comedy crudities. "To me," Spike told the *New York Times* at the time of *School Daze*'s release in March 1988, "the film is about the cosmetic differences that keep black people from coming together and being unified as a people."

True to its original title of *Homecoming*, *School Daze* opens with the massed male voices of the Morehouse Glee Club singing "I'm Building Me a Home." Throughout the opening credits, this well-chosen spiritual is heard over grainy stills from black history, including images of Malcolm X, Martin Luther King, and a very young Jesse Jackson. *School Daze* appears to be off to a terrific start, both serious and entertaining. But can it keep up this momentum?

Outside of the Mission College's administration building, Vaughan "Dap" Dunlap (Larry Fishburne), Afrocentric radical, has organized a campaign to force Mission to divest the shares it holds in corporations doing business in apartheid South Africa. The inspiring but rather judgmental and self-righteous Dap asks through a megaphone how it could be that Harvard and Princeton have divested themselves of their South African interests, but all-black Mission has not?

Dap's opposite number is Julian (Giancarlo Esposito), the slick-haired Big Man on Campus and big Brother Almighty of the Gamma Phi Gamma fraternity, a fascistic elite with an unparalleled social life and committment to endless, mindless fun. Dap and Julian square off, as they will continue to do throughout the next two hours, dragging their girlfriends Rachel Meadows (Kyme) and Jane Toussaint (Tisha Campbell), and most of the student body as well, into their confrontations.

Spike sets up the conflict between the two men (and their followers) in a rather ham-fisted fashion when Julian, the chief "Black Greek," flatly states, "We of Gamma Phi Gamma do not agree with your *African* mumbo jumbo." The curled-lipped contempt with which Esposito enunciates *African* permits no misinterpretation: more than a Wannabe, Julian's an Already Is. (Spike isn't too interested in any back-to-Africa movement personally. He may visit Senegal, and he may honor and respect the home continent, but he realizes that relocating there—either by himself or *en masse*—is just not a realistic proposition for the American born.)

Spike himself shows up as Half-Pint, a cousin of Dap's with no interest in politics. Half-Pint's only goal is to "pledge," to be accepted by Julian into the exclusive G Phi G brotherhood. Cousin Dap, on the other hand, goes around boasting that, unlike the Wannabees, he is "100% Zulu Masai," his shining blackness undiluted by a single drop of white blood. Rachel calls Dap "colorstruck" and confesses she has always suspected he wanted her only because she was "one of the *darkest* sisters on campus." Although Spike is careful to attribute both good and bad traits to the Jigs and the Wannabees, his sympathies plainly reside with the former. So much for the Rainbow Coalition and "the politics of inclusion."

The Gamma men, especially Julian, suspect that Half-Pint is still a virgin. This, of course, is a fatal flaw for a frat boy and must be remedied immediately. Before his pledge can be finalized, Half-Pint must prove he is a man of the world by having sex with Julian's girlfriend Jane, whom the Almighty has decided to "cut loose." After having sex with Jane in the Gamma House's "Bone Room," Half-Pint walks her home, and then runs to cousin Dap to brag about his conquest.

During the making of *School Daze*, Spike

expressed doubts about whether people would like his ending. For the most part, they didn't. The sudden shift to surrealism as Dap literally "wakes up" everyone on campus by screaming and ringing a bell is just too jarring after two hours of naturalistic filmmaking. Test audiences across the country complained that it was too abrupt and unresolved, but by then it was too late to change it.

Of course Dap wants everyone to "wake up," but perhaps there are better ways to get this across on a movie screen than by having your leading man stare directly into the lens and scream at the top of his lungs. That Spike is asking, even imploring, his viewers to awake from their "daze" is not the problem; it is commendable. The problem here is not the message, but Spike's deplorable dearth of dramatic invention in delivering it. Had he been slyly urging us to wake up *throughout* the entire movie— like a filmmaker is supposed to do—he wouldn't have needed to rush to this act of heavy-handed desperation a matter of moments before the clock runs out. Similarly, Spike tries to shoehorn-in some unsubtle speechifying about lack of black support for the United Negro College Fund and about Mission's continuing reliance on a family of local white philanthropists for its financial survival. From the tell-not-show school of screenwriting, one again suspects there must have been a more dramatically interesting way for Spike to have put his message across—calling Western Union, for instance.

Sort of a musical, sort of a comedy, and sort of a political drama, *School Daze* can't decide what it wants to be. Individual scenes are tremendously diverting—the Jigaboos versus the Wannabees in the beauty salon debating the issue of "good" and "bad" hair in the production number "Straight and Nappy" is a stand-out—but the whole thing just doesn't quite hang together, somehow. Spike spends far too much time documenting the silly and often sadistic hazing rituals of the Gammites—the ones that the filmmaker wants us to condemn. He wants to have it both ways.

Despite the concerns of college administrations about the general anti-intellectual bent of the picture, *School Daze* proved to be the best recruiting poster for enrollment that black schools have ever had. Black colleges noted a significant increase in applications the following fall: whatever damage *School Daze* may have done to the reputation of black higher education, it at least made it look attractive to potential customers. (The stay-in-school message would be taken up again in *House Party 2* and, to a lesser degree, in *Boyz N the Hood*.)

Certain moments in *School Daze* really hit home and give a glimpse of the film it might have been. When Dap is trying to convince his boys that they should pursue the divestment issue even if it means getting bounced off campus (like Spike's production was), one of Da Fellas (Eric A. Payne) objects. "What's wrong with wanting a nice job?," Payne's character (appropriately named Booker T) wants to know. "My daddy and moms slaved all their damn life to send my black ass to school. . . . I'm the first one ever in my family to go to college. Do you realize what that means? The first ever. All my family has always been sharecroppers, since slavery." Now *here* is a conflict with potential, and the actors with which to do it justice.

Another example is the scene when the school-boys go out for Kentucky Fried Chicken and have an ugly confrontation with some men from the town. The Local Yokels start sassing the Missionaries about being snobs, homosexuals, etc. Da Fellas retaliate with comments about the men's lack of sophistication, their "country 'Bama ass," and the shower caps covering their dripping jheri curls. One retorts that no matter how they may try to better themselves, "You're all niggers, and y'all gonna *be* niggers, just like us." To which Dap replies with intensity and poignance, "You're *not niggers!*" (In his next film, *Do the Right Thing*, Spike would again take up this theme: when Pino says the N-word, Mookie shoots back, "You see a nigger, you kick his ass!") Unfortunately, after this powerful and pertinent scene, it's right back to the paddles, the toilet humor, the choreography and the Alpo.

The fact is, Spike confused a lot of people with *School Daze*. With or without his alter ego Mars Blackmon, Spike was expected to continue more or less in the vein of *She's Gotta Have It*—cranking out bright, witty sex comedies from a black perspective. That scenario was clearly too limiting for someone of Spike Lee's ambitions and abilities.

As a musical, *School Daze* is certainly different. Like some love child conceived by a union of *A Soldier's Story* and *Hairspray, School Daze* is funny, funky, rude, imaginative, and politically alert. It's also rambling, episodic, chaotic, fragmentary, and ultimately frustrating. It somehow manages to have both too much action and too little plot, and is quite un-Spike-like in its lack of cohesion or singleness of purpose. Despite memorable moments, the overall impression it leaves is one of a project just slightly out of its creator's control.

The songs, some of which are quite entertaining and well-written in themselves, are *not* movie-musical music. Good jazz-inflected pop played and sung by talented performers is always a pleasure to hear, but musicals demand a certain discipline and simply won't work without it. For one thing, music for the theater or the movies places more emphasis on lyrics than does most pop—a demand to which Bill Lee's compositions have not paid adequate attention. Some of the lyrics, for instance, "Straight and Nappy (Good and Bad Hair)" are very funny, but it requires more straining to make them out than most moviegoers are prepared to do.

By trying to be nothing more than a music-video insert, "Da Butt" risks less but accomplishes more. Soon banned on several American campuses, "Da Butt" is an earthy little item beside which Dirty Dancing looks, er, pale. Spike fashioned the footage from this sequence into a moderately popular music-video for the go-go group EU, helping "Da Butt" become the best-known number from *School Daze*. (There was, at the time, the hope that the funky, Washington, D.C.-based go-go music of bands like Spike's friends in EU would catch on and become a national phenomenon. That never happened, as the unstoppable momentum of hip-hop steamrollered right over go-go. "Da Butt," in fact, may have been go-go's last gasp.)

In some ways, however, *School Daze* deserves comparison with *Animal House*. The sophomoric low jinks of the G Phi G frat brats are undoubtedly crowd pleasers, but by devoting almost half the screen time to them, Spike undercuts much of his own keen social commentary. The Gammas' predictably degrading initiation rites are, sad to say, just as stupid, sexist and sadistic as white kids'. The film's tendency toward the tasteless scrapes the bottom of the barrel when the Almigh-tee Julian dumps his girlfriend by "donating" her to the virginal initiate Half-Pint. The treatment of women as chattel is especially disturbing in a movie putatively dedicated to human dignity—one that even has the audacity to carry the motto "Uplift the race" in its credits. But Spike's direction is increasingly assured direction, and there's no question that he coaxed some charismatic performances from Larry Fishburne and Giancarlo Esposito. *School Daze* marked Spike's first time working with the great Ossie Davis, whom he had admired for years, the veteran actor cast as the preacher-like Coach Odom (an inspiration to his team even though they never win).

Critics and audiences can forgive a lot from a first-time filmmaker. There is an inbuilt goodwill toward new talent that turns a blind eye to faults, providing that talent is fresh and exciting. But this is only a one-time offer; eventually there will be a backlash. Often, that backlash comes at the time of Project Number Two.

Whatever the film's faults—and there are quite a

few—much of the more extreme critical abuse it received was undeserved. Some critics were not only uncomplimentary but actually vicious. *School Daze* took a particularly severe hammering from *New York Times* critic Janet Maslin, who questioned not only Spike's taste but also his technical expertise.

Spike did not take this lying down. Instead, he fought back in Maslin's paper's Letters page, calling her review "dangerous" and demanding that Maslin not be permitted to assess his films in the future. Whatever solid points he may have made throughout the letter were considerably undermined with the petty and childish conclusion, "I bet she can't even dance, does she have rhythm?"

Also, it was around this time that Spike's arrogance with the press, which got its start in his interviews for *She's Gotta Have It*, grew to new heights of hubris. He went on the road to chat up *School Daze* in a poor mood, because he felt he was being forced to do the publicity Columbia Pictures ought to be doing for him.

So it was in early 1988 that Spike began to give what became known as the Basketball Interviews. That was when he would sit in a hotel room, ignoring the interviewer, engrossed in the televised hoops, occasionally answering questions between slam dunks. Said one seasoned newspaper reporter who endured an uncooperative Spike that spring, "I wanted to say to him, 'Look, I'm sorry if I'm white, but I can't do much about that, so stop *fighting* me! I'm here to *help* you promote your fucking movie, remember?' "

Upon its release, the battles Spike thought he had

already fought with Morehouse started anew: the dirty laundry came out into the air again. Some black leaders felt that black folks had enough trouble getting their message across to white people without parading their intracommunity arguments across a movie screen. By this time, Spike was really tired of the whole subject and wanted to put a stop to it. "All the criticism I've ever gotten on the film was from those bourgeois, chicken-and-biscuit Negroes who say 'Why are there no positive images of Negroes? . . . Why open up a can of worms, reinforce what white people think of us?' If all my films were like the Huxtables, they'd be happy."

No, Spike's characters certainly aren't like *The Cosby Show*'s Huxtables, nor are they ever likely to be. The attacks on Cosby's squeaky-clean clan by more militant-minded Blacks have turned on the show's sidelining of touchy topics for mainstream, color-blind fun and games. In the process, the series presents what conservative Blacks approve as "positive images of Negroes." With such a wider spectrum of representation, *Cosby* might no longer be accused of trying to mislead Blacks and pacify Whites. (After all, *Cosby* is, for millions of American Whites, the only contact they ever have with American Blacks.) Spike has often said that "Black" is a very big topic, encompassing many different kinds of individuals and experiences, and that no black artist should feel confined to presenting only one viewpoint.

Yet another dispute would have to be faced, too. Having created the girl-group The Gamma Rays for his film, Spike intended to keep all rights to them for himself. They were his creation, he felt, and he could do with them as he wanted. To preserve the illusion that this was an actual group rather than just some college girls putting on a Homecoming show, Spike had not been planning on listing the women—Tisha Campbell, Jasmine Guy, Paula Brown and Angela Ali—individually in the movie's credits. It would therefore not be clear if the girls did their own singing (they did). Neither had Spike planned to identify the singers separately in the liner notes on the soundtrack album. The girls, in their black-and-silver lamé Gamma Ray gowns, remain one of the best-remembered sections of the film. Although Tisha Campbell was clearly the lead singer of the group, she earned no more than her back-up singers.

It took a lawsuit to change Spike's mind. Tisha Campbell not only played Julian's girlfriend Jane, but also did her own singing as the lead Gamma Ray. The singer-actress and her manager-mother, Mona Campbell, were unable to persuade Spike on the credit issue, so they had to get lawyers involved. In an out-of-court settlement, the Campbells' attorneys not only got Spike to list the singers individually, but also to pay $25,000 for the extra work required of Campbell as lead singer. Spike's defense team saw the weakness of their client's position and advised him to pay up.

Into Spike's journal went furious complaints about the case, and especially about having to hand over "$25,000 of my motherfucking hard-earned money." Contrary to Spike's telling of the story, the case was less about payment than about proper credit. In movie musicals, having offscreen vocalists do the actual work is commonplace. With The Gamma Rays, however, that was not the case, and they wanted what was owed them in the way of attribution.

"People are really going to be surprised when they find out that the girls who performed the songs in the movie actually recorded [them]," Spike wrote in *Uplift the Race*. People might be less surprised if the filmmaker took care that his movie and soundtrack credits were clear and accurate about who did what. More important than the megalomania and need for control this suggests, the incident poses questions about the substance of Spike's frequent boasts about promoting young black talent. Is *this* Spike's idea of how to get gifted Blacks into the entertainment business—by refusing to grant them simple credit for the artistic contributions they made to his movie?

School Daze rivals *Jungle Fever* for the title of Spike Lee movie with the least Spike Lee—his role as Half-Pint is more modest than his scene-stealing turn as Mars in *She's Gotta Have It*. (He gets ninth billing in *School Daze*.) It's just one more reason why watching *Daze* is an underwhelming experience; Spike's onscreen charisma is sorely missed.

"I'm definitely not going back to Columbia Pictures with [*Do the Right Thing*]," Spike wrote in his diary in the early months of 1988. "It was ideal with David Puttnam and David Picker, but . . . Steely Dawn, forget about it."

At the movie's Los Angeles opening, a nineteen-year-old South Central L.A. boy named John Singleton finally got to meet his hero Spike Lee—who had replaced his previous hero, Steven Spielberg. Little did Spike suspect that, within three years, this teenager would make *Boyz N The Hood*.

Viewed today, *School Daze* is an entertaining failure. Spike fails in a way the truly talented often fail—by promising more than he can deliver. The failure derives not from a lack of ideas, but from a surfeit of them. As Spike himself assessed in *Uplift the Race* (perhaps tacitly admitting his second feature's lack of cohesion), "*School Daze* isn't really a musical piece. But it's not a comedy or a drama either. *School Daze* is a complex hybrid of all the above. It's a hard film to describe in a sentence." Or in a paragraph, for that matter.

School Daze stands as a minor work by a major director and is, therefore, an important step in Spike's development as an artist. Besides being a timely reminder that "people of color" aren't all the same color and of the many shades between black and white, it's also fascinating as a kind of blueprint for what he would be doing over the next few years. Many of Spike's future themes are found here: class animosity (*Do the Right Thing*), light versus dark skins (*Jungle Fever*), and Blacks' dependence on help from Whites' beneficence (*The Autobiography of Malcolm X*).

In his acclaimed collection of essays, *The Content of Our Character*, California academic Shelby Steele notes that black colleges enroll only 16 percent of America's black students, but graduate 37 percent of them—a rate better than twice that of primarily white, integrated institutions. Black students on primarily white campuses drop out at a rate alarmingly higher than their white counterparts. If Spike ever decides to go "back to school" in a future film, these are issues he could consider addressing.

Every once in a while, Spike will drop one of those revealing tidbits that help us see him the way he sees himself. In assessing the pros and cons of the different studios, Spike has commented: "And since Paramount Communications Inc. owns the Knicks, I might finally get the season tickets to games I need *and deserve*" [emphasis added]. *Want*, sure. *Need*, maybe. But *deserve*? Stardom was surely setting in.

From a financial standpoint, Spike managed to do quite a bit with his $5.8 million budget—a very reasonable price for a location-shoot musical with full-scale production numbers and a couple of semi-famous names. Whatever limitations the director felt at post-Puttnam Columbia, a film of *School Daze*'s scope clearly could not have been made for the $4 million Island had to offer. Regardless of how it was promoted, *School Daze* finally returned a respectable $15 million. Moreover, in a slow 1988, it became Columbia's top-grossing picture of the year. Spike, needless to say, was of the opinion that it could have done better still, but felt vindicated. But he was also sufficiently embittered that he wanted to try working somewhere else.

Chapter 7

1988–89:
Courting Controversy

"I just think black people need to wake up. It's no coincidence that those were the last words in *School Daze* and the first in *Do the Right Thing. Wake up!*"

So said Spike Lee in a characteristically pugnacious interview with the *Washington Post* on June 30, 1989—the day the filmmaker released *Do the Right Thing*. Spike was on the interview circuit, promoting his third and most explosive film—and, of course, himself. At least in the first case, the product he was selling was solid.

Do the Right Thing was fast becoming Spike Lee's most important film to date. Even before it had been shown to the public, *Right Thing* was the most hotly debated movie of the year. Everyone who had seen it was either praising or reviling it in the strongest possible terms.

Since May 1989, when his celluloid time bomb had fragged the old guard at the 42nd annual Cannes

International Film Festival, *Do the Right Thing* had been dogged by accusations of race-baiting and riot-inciting. At Cannes, several (white) American journalists had called it inflammatory and irresponsible—some even made ominous predictions that the movie would set off a long, hot summer of political violence in New York City. For the weeks between Cannes and the June 30th release, Spike had flown back to the United States, shuttling between his New York headquarters and Los Angeles, Washington, D.C., Houston and Atlanta. In a public relations cyclone, the director was talking to anyone who'd listen, ceaselessly defending his film from the hostile critics and, in his inimitable fashion, making a host of new enemies.

But if, after today, Spike Lee never made another film in his life, *Do the Right Thing* could happily stand as his masterpiece. It regularly appears on the same lists with such films of Spike's idol Martin Scorsese as *Raging Bull* and *GoodFellas* as one of the most important American movies of the 1980s. *Do the Right Thing* is not only Spike Lee's most far-reaching and worldly effort, it also comes the closest to summing up his thoughts on the subject of race relations. Although fiercely local and specific in its references to the Bedford-Stuyvesant district of Brooklyn, it cleverly makes a single neighborhood on a single block of a single borough serve as a microcosm of an entire nation. This is why, though the action never moves off the street, the film's scope seems wider.

To understand how *Right Thing* achieved its exalted status, we need to back up a bit and look at what went into it. In early 1988, several disparate elements were coming to boil in the pressure cooker of Spike's mind. These diverse components included a Harlem riot of the 1940s, a Hollywood movie of the 1950s, a TV show of the 1960s, childhood memories—and recent real-life racial incidents in New York. It is the last of these—in particular a racially motivated death known as the Howard Beach incident—that most people assume was the basis of *Do the Right Thing*. But there is far more to this rich, resonant work than mere docudrama or agit-prop.

Race relations are, Spike says, "America's biggest problem, always has been (since we got off the boat), always will be." In Howard Beach, a working-class section of Queens, the continuing climate of mistrust between black and white Americans manifested itself as young white thugs ran out of a local pizzeria wielding baseball bats, chasing three innocent young black men out of "their" neighborhood. Figuring black males in their neighborhood could only be making trouble, the Whites hounded the three Blacks until one of them, Michael Griffith, fled into the traffic of the Belt Parkway where he was killed by a car. The incident became a rallying point in the black community, provoking the largest black rallies New York had seen since the Civil Rights movement of the 1960s. Howard Beach—or "Coward Beach" in Spikespeak—is "what made me do this movie. And that's why it has a pizzeria setting, the Italian American-Black conflict [and] the death of a young black male."

Although this and other shameful episodes in the city's recent past may have provided the political basis for his story, Spike has added his own artistic and personal touches. In the *Do the Right Thing* book he recalled "seeing a TV show when I was very young—I'm not sure if it was *Twilight Zone, Alfred Hitchcock*, or *One Step Beyond*—about a scientist who had noticed that the murder rate goes up when the temperature gets above 95 degrees. Throughout the show, the director kept showing the thermometer rising up the 90s. When it hit 95, the scientist was himself murdered." Accordingly, the characters in *Do the Right Thing* are constantly complaining about the insufferable heat—reinforced by the sweaty reds, yellows and oranges of the color scheme.

Another instance of recycling is Radio Raheem's gold knuckle-duster rings that read LOVE on one hand and HATE on the other. Spike has admitted this is his affectionate tribute to Robert Mitchum's tattooed knuckles in Charles Laughton's classic 1955 thriller *The Night of the Hunter*. "It was around the time that guys were starting to wear four-knuckle gold rings that spelled their names, so I thought, Why not have them reading LOVE and HATE?" he explains. Similarly, Raheem's soliloquy about the metaphysical prizefight between love and hate is a B-boy paraphrasing of what screenwriter James Agee had put in Mitchum's mouth three decades earlier.

A couple of other moments in the film owe credit to Malcolm X—credit he was never given. Near the end of *Do the Right Thing*, after the mob has burned Sal's Famous Pizza, they turn their anger on the Korean deli across the street. The shopkeeper fights them off by insisting that he, too, is Black. The crowd laughs, and relents from their intention of razing the shop. This memorable scene is not a particularly original one. On page 114 of *The Auto-biography of Malcolm X*, Malcolm recalls a Harlem riot during World War Two that resulted when white police shot a black soldier. While Harlemites were rampaging through the area's white businesses, "We laughed about the scared little Chinese whose restaurant didn't have a hand laid on it, because the rioters just about convulsed laughing when they saw the sign the Chinese had hastily stuck on his front door: 'Me Colored Too.' "

There's more Malcolm when Bed-Stuy kids drench the middle-aged white man's Cadillac convertible with water from the fire hydrant. When the cops question the witnesses about who did it, the old man known as Da Mayor (Ossie Davis) cryptically replies, "Those that'll tell don't know, and those that know won't tell." This, for those who know their Malcolm X, recalls page 241 of the *Autobiography*: "Whoever tells you how many Muslims there are doesn't know, and whoever does know will never tell you."

Another, more personal episode from Spike's own childhood made it to the script. When Eddie, the little boy in pursuit of an ice-cream truck, charges across a street in the path of an oncoming car, he's re-enacting a near-catastrophe Spike himself survived as a youngster in Brooklyn. "When I was a kid, I ran after an ice-cream truck and was almost hit by a speeding car," confesses Spike. "A neighbor ran into the street and snatched me from in front of the car in the nick of time. I ran home as fast as I could, crying up a storm."

As recently as February 1988, Spike was still collecting *Right Thing* material from his own life. In his corner store in Fort Greene, Spike's Joint, Spike heard an old Italian man ridicule an employee's Run-DMC tape as "jungle music." The writer would soon transmute this into the climactic confrontation between Sal and Radio Raheem in the pizzeria. Sal insists that Raheem "turn that jungle music off. We ain't in Africa," to which Buggin' Out challenges, "Why it gotta be about jungle music and Africa?"

After working out his story on index cards, one per scene, throughout that February, Spike began typing them up and fleshing them out into a complete script. Throughout March 1988, Spike called up these and other memories as he banged out his vision with his usual furious determination. By the 16th of the month, after fifteen days of intense work, he finished the first draft. He vowed that the finished product would clock in at a short, sharp, shocking ninety minutes flat. Its eventual running time would be a full one-third longer than his prediction: exactly two hours.

Spike also spent some time considering which parts should go to which actors. In the end, he used most of the people he planned on—though almost none in the roles for which he was planning. Matt Dillon, whom Spike considered for one of Sal's sons, instead chose to make *Drugstore Cowboy* with Gus Van Sant. And it was a major disappointment for the director when Robert De Niro, whom he had in mind when he created Sal, eventually passed on the offer, commenting that he'd played that kind of character too many times before.

On April 11, Spike took a break from his single-minded devotion to spend the day shooting a TV commercial for Jesse Jackson's presidential campaign. Using a volunteer crew, Spike and company worked for no pay—perhaps to return the favor Jackson did for Spike when he came to the *School Daze* set to pray for a smooth shoot. Like Spike's Public Enemy music video, campaign work for Jackson was more a labor of love than a career move.

Meanwhile, negotiations with Paramount finally proved fruitless. After being interested for several weeks, the studio eventually backed out on the idea. Not surprisingly, their executives cited the ending as problematic and unnecessarily provocative. By this time, however, Spike was getting to know his way around Hollywood and had also shopped his script to rival Universal Pictures. "The same weekend Paramount said no," he recalls, "Universal said yes."

By the 25th of May, Spike had finally cut a deal with Universal for $6.5 million, of which a significant portion would go to the unions. After having looked for between $7 and $10 million, the tightness of the budget was a blow: to make *Do*, Spike would have to make do. Of this he was more than slightly resentful: "White boys get real money, fuck up, lose millions of dollars, and still get chance after chance. Not so with us. You fuck up one time, that's it." Here, the man has a point. But what he may not realize is that this challenge, though difficult, has also driven him to be better and stronger. Around this time Spike proudly pointed out to *Rolling Stone*, "I go directly to Hollywood for my money," as opposed to raising small sums here and there, the way most independents must—and the way Spike himself did in the early days. For someone still operating outside the studio system, Spike Lee can probably arrange financing more easily than anyone else.

After a six-week prep, Spike began an eight-week shoot on Brooklyn's Stuyvesant Avenue, between Lexington and Quincy. It lasted from July 18 through September 9. To show their goodwill to the community, the production threw a block party just before shooting started. There, Spike, Monty Ross and guest of honor Melvin Van Peebles stressed the importance of the endeavor to the neighborhood and asked for their cooperation. Spike also spoke at the local school (where *Right Thing*'s extras passed the time between shots).

Tagging along was a film crew led by documentarist St. Clair Bourne, who produced the enjoyable (if not particularly revealing) sixty-minute film, *The Making of "Do the Right Thing."* A fairly standard behind-the-scenes look, *The Making of . . .* was unlikely to reveal anything controversial, as it was a coproduction between Bourne's Chamba Organization and 40 Acres. As valuable as Bourne's documentary undoubtedly is, it should be remembered that it was commissioned only as an electronic press kit (EPK)—the video documentaries that production companies now commonly make to hype a movie's release, from which TV shows such as *Entertainment Tonight*, can pull clips. *The Making of "Do the Right Thing"* is an interesting look at Spike Lee at work, but to try to pass it off as a documentary with an independent point of view, or as educational television (where it sometimes turns up), isn't quite honest.

It is, however, the only kind of documentation or analysis of his work that Spike Lee will tolerate: one that is indistinguishable from advertising. *The Making of . . .* never probes very deeply, instead taking Spike at his word on everything. The only moment of dissent is when a resident of the block on which the crew was shooting complains that the inconveniences to everyday life presented by the shoot are greater than the production had led them to believe—and therefore he felt entitled to more compensation than the production had paid him.

Much of *Do the Right Thing*'s strength derives from Spike's decision to shoot on location. "I would have been *crucified*," Spike exclaims, "if I made a movie about Bed-Stuy and not shot it there." Despite claiming deep affection for the bedraggled district, he's on record as calling Bed-Stuy "a tense and hostile environment." Spike also felt the neighborhood required security beyond the usual rent-a-cops and bored Barnes men. Instead, the director courted controversy yet again by hiring the Fruit of Islam, Minister Louis Farrakhan's own private security force. Trained in self-defense, the Fruit, in their snappy suits and signature bow ties, are the business end of the Nation of Islam, the militant Black Muslim organization on whose behalf Malcolm X once raged. Spike had pulled off a PR coup that outdid Mick Jagger's notorious use of Hell's Angels as counterculture cops at an outdoor Rolling Stones concert in California twenty years earlier.

Despite their ability to terrify white America more than any motorcycle gang, the Fruit of Islam's presence in Bed-Stuy was peaceful and productive. And, unlike Jagger's biker buddies, Minister Farrakhan's men did not kill any of the people they were hired to protect. In an instance of genuine service to the community, the ferociously anti-drug Fruit boarded up two crack dens in abandoned buildings and chased the dealers off the block. Although they were unable to put the pushers out of business altogether, they at least forced them to keep moving.

The rest of the *Do the Right Thing* crew also tried to do the right thing by the neighborhood, making an effort to involve locals and bring (at least temporary) employment to the community. As he would later do in Harlem on the *Jungle Fever* shoot, Spike even gave a gofer position to a transient woman prone to wandering off on crack binges.

Bed-Stuy has families that go back 125 years— back to the Emancipation Proclamation, in fact— on the same street, with a strong sense of community the production knew had to be respected. By the end of the shoot, the block of Stuyvesant Avenue was memorialized both by a plaque laid in the sidewalk and by renaming the street: alongside the sign reading STUYVESANT AVE hung a new one, DO THE RIGHT THING AVE. Neither plaque nor sign stands today; overzealous souvenir collectors have stolen both of them.

Over the winter of 1988–89, Spike supervised the editing and sound-mixing of *Do the Right Thing* from his 40 Acres and a Mule's Filmworks headquarters. The goal was to finish in time for the Cannes Festival in May.

The film caused a disturbance right from its first screening, with some of the more hysterical journalists from the United States going so far as to predict race riots. The three main prophets of doom were David Denby of *New York* magazine, Richard "Take a hike, Spike" Corliss of *Time*, and Jeannie "I don't need this movie in New York this summer!" Williams, *USA Today*'s gossip columnist. Williams went on to blurt out in front of other reporters such alarmist hysteria as "I don't know what they're thinking! What's going to happen when they *release* this?"

Finally, Spike strode into a Cannes press conference wearing his MALCOLM X: NO SELLOUT T-shirt. Spike explained he specifically wanted a summer release because "in November there's going to be an election for mayor of New York, and Koch has divided the city into black and white." (The following September, Mayor Ed Koch stepped out of the race, leaving it up to Rudy Giuliani to challenge—and eventually lose to—black candidate David Dinkins.) "If anything happens," Spike said later in the press conference, "it'll be because the cops killed somebody else with no reason, but it won't be because of *Do the Right Thing*."

Most filmmakers recoil at the idea of explaining their work. Not Spike—he's only too happy to interpret himself for his audience. "Ultimately," he philosophizes, "this film is about whether we are going to make an effort to live together. I hope when people look at my film they will ask themselves this question: 'Am I any of those people in the movie? And, if I am, how can I change myself for the better?' " (*Daily News*, June 25, 1989).

Presumably, that goes for Blacks and Whites and all points between. Certainly, there are few characters who couldn't use some kind of improving.

"What's the difference between Hollywood characters and my characters?" asks Spike later in the *News* interview. "Mine are real."

But he also knows his limitations as an interpreter of his own work and, contrary to popular opinion, sometimes knows when to quit. He explained the situation to *Premiere* magazine. "People come to *Do the Right Thing* and say, 'Spike, give us the answer to race relations.' I can't do that." That, he says, "would be abusing the medium of film." In fact, he says his "number one concern as a black filmmaker is to try to be the best filmmaker you can, first and foremost to learn your craft"—words he does not always live by. Usually, of course, Spike is stating the case for ideologically committed art and against the "bourgeois formalism" of "art for art's sake." Except, of course, when it suits him.

More fireworks went off when questioning at the conference turned to Alan Parker's recently released *Mississippi Burning*. Spike expressed his displeasure in no uncertain terms: "*Hated* it!" He argued, as have many others, that the deaths of three civil rights workers had been reduced to a conventional Hollywood thriller that presented FBI agents (played by Gene Hackman and Willem Dafoe) as heroes, reducing Blacks to extras in their own history. "They should have had the guts to have at least one central black character," Spike spat.

Spike's press conference had certainly warmed things up that chilly, rainy Cannes spring but, like *Do the Right Thing*'s thermometer, the heat wave was not over yet. Spike had been boasting up and down the Croisette that he expected to win the festival's top prize, the Palme d'Or, and that there'd be hell to pay if he didn't. He didn't. German director Wim Wenders (*Paris, Texas*) headed the jury at the Cannes Festival and was instrumental in the festival's decision against *Do the Right Thing*.

Wenders is an artstruck Euroweenie whose concerns are with the individual and not with society as a whole. His approach is psychological; Spike's is sociological. Wenders was quoted as saying that Mookie's tossing the garbage can through the pizzeria window was "an unheroic act." Instead, the jury favored Steve Soderbergh's erotic comedy-drama *sex, lies and videotape*. When Spike got wind of Wenders' rationale for awarding the Palme d'Or to *sex, lies*, he sneered, "James Spader watching videos and masturbating—yeah, *very heroic*!"

Never a good loser, Spike's reaction was to erupt publicly by accusing the jury of rigging and bigotry. "We got robbed, gypped, jerked around—they gave us the okey-doke" (*Washington Post*, June 30, 1989). Although he has said he enjoyed *sex, lies*, Spike made it plain he felt Soderbergh's film took the prize because the director wasn't Black. Worse, he threatened Wim Wenders, saying he better watch out because he'd be "waiting for his ass" and that "Somewhere deep in my closet I have a Louisville Slugger baseball bat with Wenders's name on it."

All this was, of course, widely reported in the American media. Spike may not have taken home the festival's top honors, but he came away with something more valuable: acres of ink as columnists across the United States argued back and forth that *Do the Right Thing* was or was not racist, did or did not advocate violence, was or was not a major work of art. Weeks before it was scheduled to open, *Do the Right Thing* was the talk of the movie world, more eagerly awaited in some quarters than the multimillion-dollar *Batman*.

Ironic foreshadowing to all this feuding can be found in the notes Spike scribbled to himself about his own character, Mookie. "Mookie is an instigator, a rabble-rouser," Spike wrote in his *Do the Right Thing* book. "He's a cantankerous person, always on the offensive. Mookie loves to start arguments. He should be arguing the entire movie. He's small but he has the mouth to back it up."

Sound like anyone you know?

Chapter 8

Do or Die:
A Whine of the Times

I just saw Spike Lee's latest film, Do the Right
Thing, *and I thought, how blessed this young
man is,* not *to have been born in 1905, or 1915,
or 1925, or even 1935.*

—DICK CAMPBELL, *Amsterdam News,*
(July 15, 1989)

"Timing is everything" is a cliche beloved by the
entertainment industry. With *Do the Right Thing,*
Spike Lee's timing couldn't have been better. For
the summer of 1989, Spike Lee was the man of the
moment. *Batman* may have done bigger business,
but not even Michael Keaton was associated with
that film by moviegoers the way Spike was identified
with *Do the Right Thing.*

Having lit the flames at Cannes, Spike then fanned
them for the five weeks left until the film's June 30
release date. "I know there will be an uproar about

this one," said Spike in the *Daily News*. "I wouldn't be surprised if 40 Acres and a Mule receives death threats."

Even if the situation never got quite so far as death threats, things got uncomfortably tense just the same. Spike went into pit-bull mode, apparently following the dictum, Don't defend, offend. As the movie hit the screen, Spike was feuding with many a media luminary. He even argued that what happens in the film's climax was not a riot but an uprising.

And once the American public could actually see the film, these arguments became ballistic. Spike's Cannes controversies had made for shocking copy and the kind of publicity not even payola can buy. But they were just the beginning: the fires Spike started in May were still blazing in September.

In the case of *Do the Right Thing*, more than any other Spike Lee joint, it is important to review exactly the facts and figures of the situation: with a film as contentious as this, there are enough ways to get into an argument without being misinformed.

Time: The present, on the hottest day of summer.

Place: A block in the Bedford-Stuyvesant section of Brooklyn comprising, in Spike's terms, "the black and Puerto Rican underclass."

Mood: Ugly.

First up is the jive-talking deejay Mister Señor Love Daddy (Sam Jackson) at WE-LOVE who knows the score; he warns that the forecast is *hot*, and warns jheri-curl users to stay inside or risk "a permanent plastic helmet on yo' head for*ever*!"

Sal (Danny Aiello), the beefy middle-aged patriarch of Sal's Famous Pizzeria, pulls up in his massive Eldorado with his two sons, Pino (John Turturro) and Vito (Richard Edson). Pino leads off a brief expository conversation about how he hates the neighborhood. Sal laments that the shop's air-conditioning is still broken, because he can't convince the repairman to visit Bed-Stuy without a police escort. Mister Señor Love Daddy has announced that it's hot; we now see that things will only get hotter.

Next appears the star of our show, Mookie (Spike Lee): brother to Jade (Joie Lee), some-time boyfriend to Tina (Rosie Perez), absentee father to Hector, and delivery lad to Sal. In Jade's apartment, Mookie wakes up his screen sis by climbing into her bed and playing with her lips with his fingers. Later, Spike the actor defends her honor in a confrontation Spike the writer invented. He also shows her showering. (For those of a Freudian persuasion, the film is a field day.)

Mookie slouches off down the block to work, resplendent in his diamond earring, fashionable fade, and Dodgers number 42 baseball shirt (in honor of barrier-breaking ballplayer Jackie Robinson). He barks a curt "Hell, no!" to a couple of Jehovah's Witnesses peddling *The Watchtower*. In the restaurant, a shabby but genteel old man who likes to be called Da Mayor (Ossie Davis) asks if Sal wants his storefront swept. Pino's unsolicited advice is that Mookie could do this, so why hand over good money to an *azzupepe* (Italian slang meaning, roughly, "lazy black bum"). Without knowing what has been said, Mookie steps into the fray: "Da Mayor ain't no *azzupepe*!"

A little later, we see Da Mook deliver pizzas in the insolent manner he perhaps imagines will bring him tips. In his sluggish, sloppy comportment, Spike's Mookie is about as far as one can get from the athletic grace of his namesake, then New York Met (and current Toronto Blue Jay) Mookie Wilson.

Buggin' Out (Giancarlo Esposito), a regular customer at the pizzeria, hassles Sal about why, in a black neighborhood, there are only pictures of Italians and Italian-Americans on Sal's Wall of Fame. Among the 8 X 10 mug shots (including Frank Sinatra, Sophia Loren and, significantly, Robert De Niro), Buggin' wonders, should there not be some representation of African-Americans? Sal's reply is that if Buggin' wants to put up pictures of accomplished Blacks, he should get his own joint.

And the heat goes on. Just in case we haven't yet gotten the message that it's hot, Spike supplies a heat montage: ice cubes, fans, showers, set to reggae band Steel Pulse's "Can't Stand It." The sequence is one of very few in the film that isn't strictly essential to the whole (although it is not quite as gratuitous as DJ Love Daddy's lengthy voice-over cataloguing of black musical artists—pure filler in an otherwise tight, economical film).

Radio Raheem (Bill Nunn, from *School Daze*) shows up to do what he does best: glare angrily and strut around while his boom-box of the gods blasts Public Enemy's "Fight the Power" so loud as to be heard from here to Hoboken. Raheem challenges the local Spanish boys to a round of dueling ghetto-blasters, ending in a clear victory for Raheem. Such confrontations increase throughout the film until the riot—sorry, *uprising*. Meanwhile, Mookie and Vito deliver a pizza to Mister Señor Love Daddy, who invites Mookie to dedicate a song to Tina. Mookie encourages Vito to stand up to Pino's bullying and bigotry.

We drop in on a trio of street corner crotch-grabbers known as the Corner Men: Sweet Dick Willie (Robin Harris), ML (Paul Benjamin) and Coconut Sid (Frankie Faison). ML leads off a discussion about the Korean deli across the street—and why Blacks don't run their own businesses. Observing that the space now occupied sat boarded up for years, ML goes on to promise that he'd gladly patronize black business in his area—if there were any to patronize. At first, Sweet Dick Willie and Coconut Sid are skeptical, but when they think about it a little, they begin to realize ML may have a point.

"Everyone else has a business and supports their own but us," says one of the men. Here, Spike reprises a theme advanced by the elderly college deans in *School Daze*, in their discussion of the depressingly low levels at which Blacks contribute to the United Negro College Fund. It also conjures *A Raisin in the Sun*, the Lorraine Hansbury play forcefully filmed in 1961 with Sidney Poitier, Claudia McNeil, Ruby Dee, and Louis Gossett. In this classic of black Hollywood, a poor family in Chicago tries to get out of its rut when the father (Poitier) enters into a liquor store venture with untrustworthy partners. The Corner Men's economic summit ends not with a plan for action, but with Sweet Dick Willie's loping across to buy a beer from the Koreans.

Ahmad, Punchy, Cee and the crew hassle Da Mayor about his fairly consistent inebriation. Da

Mayor retaliates with stories from the bad old days, about watching helplessly as his wife and children starved. What the young 'uns should be giving him, says Da Mayor, is not sass but respect. "I respect those who respect themselves," retorts Ahmad. Again, a dilemma with no clear resolution.

In one of *Do the Right Thing*'s quieter moments, Mookie sits Pino down for a little talk about his racism. As Mookie points out, Pino (and millions of Whites like him) have no trouble dealing with Blacks who are successes in the media: Magic Johnson, Eddie Murphy and Prince are among Pino's favorite people. Pino's defense is that these stars are "not really black, they're *more* than black"—a rationalization which even he must recognize is feeble and illogical.

At this point, Spike breaks frame for the direct address, racial slurs scene: Mookie starts the ball rolling by dissing Italians (as "garlic-breath, spaghetti-bending wop," etc.). Pino retaliates with equally vicious crudity about "Moulan yans" (Italian for eggplant). Gaining momentum, an Hispanic hurls epithets at Koreans, a cop insults Hispanics, and a Korean shopkeeper cusses out Jews. (Please note that every group gets it as good as they give it— except Jews, who not only get it but are also denied equal time to respond.) In a surrealistic touch, Mr. Señor Love Daddy breaks in over the airwaves and instructs them to cut it out.

Mookie asks Sal if he can get paid early; Sal refuses. Radio Raheem does his Love and Hate soliloquy for Mookie. Pino complains (again) about Blacks: "I'm sick of niggers . . . they're like animals." Sal tries to calm down his hot-headed son:

This brownstone in Brooklyn was Spike's youthful home.
(Photo © Ron Goldberg)

After film school Spike moved into a basement apartment in this house. This apartment was the first headquarters for 40 Acres and a Mule. (Photo © Ron Goldberg)

Bill Lee's house.
Spike lived here while attending New York University.
(Photo © Ron Goldberg)

In 1985 The Ferry Bank Restaurant occupied the first floor of this building. Spike shot much of *She's Gotta Have It* on the upper floor. Note the windows which were so prominent in the film.

(Photo © Ron Goldberg)

This empty lot in Bedford-Stuyvesant was the scene of Sal's Pizzeria in *Do the Right Thing*. Spike had the Mike Tyson sign put up. (Photo © Ron Goldberg)

The Soldier's Monument in Ft. Greene Park commemorates the American prison ships during the Revolutionary War. Spike staged the *She's Gotta Have It* dance around this Brooklyn landmark. (Photo © Ron Goldberg)

Gianocarlo Esposito and Joie Lee joined Spike to celebrate the first anniversary of Spike's Joint.   (Photo © Chris Buck/Visages)

Wesley Snipes at the anniversary. (Photo © Chris Buck/Visages)

Spike's Joint

(Photo © Chris Buck/Visages)

The abandoned firehouse in Brooklyn that is now the headquarters for 40 Acres and a Mule. (Photo © Ron Goldberg)

"Sure, some of them don't like us, but most of them do."

Buggin' canvasses the street seeking signatures for his boycott of Sal's. He meets with rejection from everyone from Ahmad to Sweet Dick Willie, who advises, "Maybe what you oughta do is boycott that goddamned barber that fucked up yo' *head*." (This is invariably the picture's biggest laugh, yet one for which Spike can't take credit: not in the script, the line was an on-set improvisation by Harris himself.) Buggin' expects support from Jade. But Jade, who along with Love Daddy is the movie's voice of reason, wonders if he couldn't "direct his energies in a more useful way" to do "something positive for the community."

Sal has just finished warning Mookie about his lateness when Jade walks in and the pieman's mood improves noticeably. He is exceedingly, even sickeningly, polite to her, volunteering to make her a special sandwich. Outside, heat is visibly rising from the pavement in distorting waves as Raheem's wall-of-noise boom-box finally runs down, and he goes to Koreans for twenty D-size Energizers. Da Mayor buys flowers for Mother Sister; she's not impressed. A little later, Da Mayor saves Eddie from being crushed, and Mother Sister lightens up. Back at the pizzeria, Sal is sweet-talking Jade; Da Mook takes her outside and tells her to stay away. Mookie tells Sal to quit hitting on her; Sal denies any such intentions. Da Mayor regales Mother Sister with a tale about a memorable ballgame he once played in Snow Hill, Alabama (where Spike spent many a summer as a boy).

Mookie delivers pizza to a familiar address: his girlfriend (and mother of his child Hector) Tina. Mookie wants to use the occasion as a pit stop, but Tina warns him there'll be "no rawness jumping off today." Instead, he goes to the icebox, grabs a tray and runs the cubes over her naked body in a witty safe-sex exercise. Other than to reprimand Tina's mother for speaking Spanish to his son ("It's bad enough his name is *Hector*!"), Mookie pays no attention to the child he fathered.

In an ugly scene in Sal's back room, Pino intimidates Vito over his friendship with Mookie, warning him that no Black can be trusted. Outside, Buggin' finally finds a convert to his cause in the huge, seething form of Radio Raheem. Together, they agree to put their demands to the big guy.

Sal's about to call it a day when the street kids want four final slices. Mookie wants to go home, but Sal instructs him to let them in briefly. The kids are followed by Buggin' and Raheem, presenting their Wall of Fame ultimatum with high-decibel Public Enemy punctuation. In a fit of anger, Sal smashes Raheem's radio with a baseball bat and all hell breaks loose: punches are thrown, tables are overturned, and chairs are crashed over backs as in many a saloon brawl in many a Western. (In Westerns, however, cowboys don't usually torch the saloon.)

After the struggle has spilled out into the street, police officers arrive (with backup) to haul away Buggin' and Raheem. Struggling to get free, Raheem has his windpipe crushed in the same chokehold that killed a young black man named Michael Stewart. With a nightstick held horizontally under his chin, Radio Raheem becomes Air Raheem as he is lifted right off the ground. When Spike dives in for a close-up of Raheem's dangling Nikes, it's clear that Raheem fought the power and the power won. As his lifeless bulk is carted off in the meat wagon, the crowd turns from unruly to venomous. The ambulances and police vehicles pull out, leaving the mob unsupervised (would this really happen?). They turn to the Korean grocer as their next victim—who is spared their wrath when he pleads that he, too, is Black.

What has happened—that one of their own has died needlessly—begins to sink in. Mookie picks up a trash can and heaves it through the pizzeria's plate glass window. After that, it's open season. Smiley (Roger Smith), the well-meaning young postcard vendor with the speech impediment, pins one of his hand-tinted photos of Dr. Martin Luther King, Jr. and Malcolm X to the Wall of Fame, then strikes the match that will incinerate the premises.

This much can't be denied for *Right Thing*'s penultimate moments: Spike really knows how to create tension and visual excitement. The shooting, the cutting, all work together to create a maximum of excitement with a minimum of actual on-screen violence. Like *Psycho*'s shower sequence, we are terrified more by what we *think* we're seeing.

Ultimately, though, *Do the Right Thing* is about more than truncheon-happy cops or charred pizza. By creating an orgy of disorienting angles, lunging dolly-shots, audacious hand-helds, vibrant "Afrocentric" color scheme, it is nothing less than a panorama of contemporary urban America.

Danny Aiello was nominated for a Supporting Actor Oscar for his role as the Famous Sal himself, in what is undeniably a bravura performance. (Spike also took a nomination the following spring for Best Original Screenplay, which he, too, lost.)

Both Aiello and Spike must have wondered what they were getting into when they met and Aiello announced, "You may be a little to the left of the leftest guy I know, and I'm 150 miles to the right of Ronald Reagan. Can we work together?" They could, and did—though not without some conflicts over the interpretation of his role. Aiello wanted to make him more sympathetic and likable; Spike resisted. Eventually, they compromised—and got the complex, rich, resonant individual we now know as Sal.

In a suspiciously clean Bed-Stuy, Spike lets his camera linger on what is apparently the only graffiti in the neighborhood: the neatly lettered "Tawana told the truth." This refers to the controversy over alleged rape victim Tawana Brawley, who became a *cause célèbre* for New York Blacks in 1988 and 1989—despite her story of victimization at the hands of white thugs being widely discredited. Perhaps Spike means she "told the truth" in a metaphorical sense; that while she was dealing in fiction not fact, Tawana made important points just the same (in much the same way as a movie or novel can without being literally "true"). Spike's own comment on the situation is that we may never know the truth, but that he doesn't think what happened is something a young girl would do to herself.

Yet since the Tawana Brawley case there have been several similar bias attacks in which the plaintiffs later admitted to having concocted the stories themselves—even including radio mouthpiece Morton Downey, Jr. This, however, is not to say that there might not be something to be learned from studying these claims, which perhaps can be seen as ritualized enactments of what the victims feel is done to them every day. Viewed this way, such stories take on properties of politicized performance art.

The film's famous ending posits competing philosophies from the 1960s' two most influential black leaders, Dr. Martin Luther King, Jr. and Malcolm X.

> Violence as a way of achieving racial justice is both impractical and immoral. It is impractical because it is a descending spiral ending in destruction for all. The old law of an eye for an eye leaves everybody blind. It is immoral because it seeks to humiliate the opponent rather than win his understanding; it seeks to annihilate rather than to convert. Violence is immoral because it thrives on hatred rather than love. It destroys community and makes brotherhood impossible. It leaves society in monologue rather than dialogue. Violence ends by defeating itself. It creates bitterness in the survivors and brutality in the destroyers.
>
> DR. MARTIN LUTHER KING, JR.

> I think there are plenty of good people in America, but there are also plenty of bad people in America, and the bad ones are the ones

who seem to have all the power and be in these positions to block things that you and I need. Because this is the situation, you and I have to preserve the right to do what is necessary to bring an end to that situation, and it doesn't mean that I advocate violence, but at the same time I am not against using violence in self-defense. I don't even call it violence when it's self-defense, I call it intelligence.

MALCOLM X

Is this an appreciation of duality and of moral ambiguity we have come to expect in major artists? Maybe. Yet Spike himself isn't really so ambiguous: elsewhere, he leaves little doubt as to which side he's on. His film may end with quotes from two great Negro leaders, but his published script begins with only one:

The greatest miracle Christianity has achieved in America is that the black man in white Christian hands has not grown violent. It *is* a miracle that 22 million black people have not *risen up* against their oppressors—in which they would have been justified by all moral criteria, and even by the democratic tradition! It is a miracle that a nation of black people has so fervently continued to believe in a turn-the-other-cheek and heaven-for-you-after-you-die philosophy! It *is* a *miracle* that the American Black people have remained a peaceful people, while catching all the centuries of hell that they have caught, here in the white man's heaven! The *miracle* is that the white man's puppet

Negro 'leaders', his preachers and the educated
Negroes laden with degrees, and others who
have been allowed to wax fat off their black
poor brothers, have been able to hold the black
masses quiet until now.

This passage, from *The Autobiography of
Malcolm X*, is clearly close to Spike's heart—
and even reminiscent of Buggin' Out's loaded
line, "You're lucky the black man has a kind
and loving heart." Spike even says himself, "The
character I play [in *Do the Right Thing*] is from
the Malcolm X school of thought: 'An eye for an
eye.' "

At least sometimes, however, Spike displays what
appears to be a genuine intent to be fair and honest:
"It can't be just a diatribe, WHITE MAN THIS,
WHITE MAN THAT" [capitalization in original],
he wrote in an early note to himself. And, just a
couple of lines down on the same page, "I know I'll
come up against some static from the white press.
They'll say I'm trying to incite a race riot"
(emphasis added).

Back in the *She's Gotta Have It* days, Spike was
compared to Woody Allen, although for largely
superficial reasons (height, spectacles, Brooklyn,
etc.). Here, however, a more meaningful comparison
with Allen can be drawn: the two men share a will-
ingness to leave their films open-ended. In *Crimes
and Misdemeanors*, Martin Landau's character "gets
away with" the killing of his bothersome mistress.
Legally, he may have been let off the hook; morally
he was sentenced to carry his guilty secret with him
for the rest of his days. Like the cryptic finale of *Do*

the Right Thing, this is something film fans can argue about for hours.

America's most prominent critics did just that. Richard Shickel in *Time* (July 3, 1989), after a somewhat admiring review, turned quite nasty at the end: "The morning after igniting the riot, Mookie slinks back to demand that Sal pay him his week's wages. Behind the camera, Lee wants the same thing: to create a riot of opinion, then blame viewers for not getting the message he hasn't bothered to articulate." It gets worse: Schickel concludes with "Even Mister Señor Love Daddy might say, 'Take a hike, Spike!'"—a cheap joke unworthy of someone of Schickel's reputation. Furthermore, "Lee will not be ingratiating; he wants to be accepted on his own rude terms. Same goes for *Do the Right Thing*." And, "A few fear that *Do the Right Thing* could trigger the kind of riot it dramatizes *and perhaps condones*" [emphasis added].

Spike also did not get much support from the other important weekly, *Newsweek*: two reviews, one for and one against. David Ansen praised *Right Thing*, while Jack Kroll condemned it as "an evasion of the issues." Invoking the imagery of terrorism, Kroll charged that the film places "dynamite under every seat." And Stanley Crouch, a black journalist unimpressed with Spike's brand of militancy, even invoked the word "fascism" in one of eight(!) stories *The Village Voice* devoted to the film.

As early as March of 1988, Spike made journal entries about how studios are "scared that this film might incite Black folks to riot. Needless to say, I don't agree with them." In 1989, he would elaborate, "It's racist to assume black people can't distinguish between what's real and what's on the screen. What frightens people is that what's in the movie is reality." And, "People don't need my films to make them angry. My films are designed to provoke thought and discussion about the number-one issue in my eyes: racism. People are under the impression that racism is gone, dormant, a thing of the past. . . . It's cops killing innocent black people. *That's* what makes a riot" (*Washington Post*, June 30, 1989).

In a rare moment of modesty, Spike said around this time, "I still do not consider myself an actor. I do OK." But just let someone *else* try to suggest that, and Spike's ready to go to bat again. In August of that year, a white fan approached Spike to compliment his directing but complain about his acting, saying "I think you should keep directing, but don't put yourself in your films anymore. Your acting just doesn't live up to your directing." Spike's reaction? Get out the Louisville Slugger: "Do me a favor," he told the crowd. "Hit this guy over the head with a baseball bat."

Despite his modest estimation of his own on-screen abilities, Spike continues to put himself in his own movies mainly for commercial reasons—not only because it saves on the payroll, but because he recognizes that he's personally popular and therefore a box-office draw. *Right Thing*'s own box-office takings were handsome: over $25 million, making it by far the most profitable Spike Lee film to date and causing an industry insider to exclaim that "Spike is as big as Eddie Murphy in New York now." Even so, Spike felt the film could have done better had the squeamish critics not scared off potential white customers with prophecies of doom.

Come September, the stifling summer was abating. But *Do the Right Thing* was still playing—and so was Spike. That month, Spike told the left-leaning glossy *Mother Jones* about the erstwhile affable Mookie's tossing of the trash can: "People don't like the fact that it's Spike Lee who starts it," he says, starting to slip into the dangerous (and often fatal) celebrity habit of referring to oneself in the third person. "They feel cheated and tricked. That's the one black character that they liked. But Mookie had to act. Everybody did."

And Giancarlo Esposito says of his part in *Right Thing*, "I don't think what happens to Buggin' Out is resolved. That's another picture. I think a lot of it is another picture as far as Spike Lee endings go. The other picture is in your brain. You must resolve it yourself."

Spike had intended from the beginning that *Do the Right Thing*'s "script should be and will be more experimental than *School Daze*, a lot more like *She's Gotta Have It*." And it is: with the montages and especially the racial slur segment, we see him stretching as a filmmaker. But unlike the stabs Spike made at bending the form of film in *She's Gotta Have It*, his reach no longer exceeded his grasp. He had finally progressed with his art to the point that getting his vision out of his head and onto the screen was no longer left to chance.

But as much as *Right Thing* may conjure the textures and attitudes of its locale, Spike's Bed-Stuy is not completely believable. It may be unfair to ask "Where are the drugs?" but it is not unfair to ask "Where is the graffiti?" A big red wall without a single tag sprayed or scrawled on it? When had it been repainted—that morning?

A comment by Sheila Benson of the *Los Angeles Times* must have made Spike Lee very happy. After endless (and not particularly imaginative) comparisons to Melvin Van Peebles and Woody Allen, someone finally invoked the name of Spike's *real* hero: "There's something seditious and Scorsese-like about *Do the Right Thing*."

Do the Right Thing is the director's most ambitious, most satisfying film to date, an incendiary, forceful and persuasive piece of work. It is also (it must be said) a *stressful* movie to sit through. But, in the way of most great art, the short-term discomfort it may cause is of the ameliorative kind: by showing what *could* happen, it may even help society to prevent precisely such occurrences in the future.

With his first two films, Spike Lee became a player. But *She's Gotta Have It* and *School Daze* were both comedies—and as popular or as critically acclaimed as classic comedies might be, critics still tend to consider them lightweight. Dramas are where a filmmaker must really prove himself as a serious artist. "WE LOVE." "LOVE and HATE." "Are we gonna live together? Together are we gonna live?" These are serious themes, artfully woven into the fabric of the story.

Regardless of which side one is on, everyone takes *Do the Right Thing* seriously. Very seriously. In fact, *almost* as seriously as Mr. Lee takes himself. Like Malcolm's phrase, "By any means necessary," *Right Thing* isn't necessarily an endorsement of violence, but rather a warning that Blacks will not forever endure persecution passively. In a perverse way, the film might even be seen as a cautionary tale.

In the closing credits, Spike dedicates the picture "to the families of Eleanor Bumpurs, Michael Griffith, Arthur Miller, Edmund Perry, Yvonne Smallwood, Michael Stewart." And, we might add, Yusef Hawkins. Ironically, the accompanying music is the velvety voice of Al Jarreau crooning "Never Explain Love." What *Do the Right Thing* leaves unexplained is not love, but hatred.

Chapter 9

Sensible Shoes, Senseless Violence, and Other Commercial Considerations

From the first time Mars Blackmon rode in with his razor-cut fade, Spike Lee has been associated with fashion trends. During prep for *Do the Right Thing*, Spike realized that to go with existing 1988 fashions, he would automatically be out of date when the picture opened twelve months later. His goal became not to reproduce what was already hot on the street, but to predict what might look hot the following summer. He guessed well: the summer of 1989 saw millions of young people wearing Mookie-style surfer baggies over lycra bike shorts.

Spike's films not only reflect contemporary clothing and styles, but also affect and influence them. No other filmmaker has been so closely identified with street fashion and the commercial world. But then, as an outspoken proponent of black entrepreneurship, no filmmaker has had more justification for participating in it.

And clothes aren't all. It would eventually become apparent that nothing less than his own store would be able to cope with all the Spike-related products that his movies tend to generate. No other director in history has had a store devoted to his own spin-offs, an achievement that makes Spike Lee the Menudo of the film world. What usually fascinates the general public is not movie makers, but movie *stars*. Few directors have ever achieved such widespread recognition that fans would, for instance, stop them on the street for autographs—a select list probably limited to Alfred Hitchcock, Woody Allen, and Spike Lee. (What these three have in common—besides excelling in their craft—is that they appeared in their own films.)

In a brilliant exercise in cross-promotion, Lee opened Spike's Joint at One South Elliott Place in Fort Greene in September of 1990. *Mo' Better Blues* had been in (and left) theaters that summer, bringing the number of promotable films in the Spike Lee repertoire to four. The store, he figured, would not only keep control of his movie-related merchandise in the family, but the merchandise would, in turn, help to publicize the movies—so that Spike really couldn't lose regardless of whether or not the place turned a profit.

"Films are only an excuse for me to design T-shirts," Spike once laughed. But take a walk through Spike's Joint in Brooklyn and you'll wonder if he was really joking. Spike's Joint is proof that Spike

Lee is more than a filmmaker; he's a one-man cottage industry.

To its proprietor's credit, Spike's Joint is not a tourist trap, but one of the cleanest, most tasteful operations in its area. And Spike practices quality control over the merchandise that bears his name—Mars Blackmon lunchboxes, for instance, were not on the menu. It must also be said that Spike's not afraid to *charge* for all this. His stuff is good, but it's not cheap, either: a humble T-shirt can be $25, and a leather/fabric Malcolm X jacket will set you back $350. Postcards, videos, books and even bolo ties featuring small faces of Spike's rogues' gallery of characters molded of clay are also offered for sale.

Spike's Joint had another, more honorable reason for opening apart from the stroking of its owner's ego: to promote the idea of black-owned businesses. As a successful filmmaker, Spike is already a living example of the African-American bootstrap capitalism he endorses. Alas, not everyone can be that, as the talent to become an *auteur* is rare. But self-employed businessperson is a goal attainable by many. On the opening of the Joint, the *Village Voice*'s Nelson George wrote "Spike's subversion of entertainment industry orthodoxy in favor of economic nationalism may prove to be his most enduring legacy." Yet Spike's mingling of materialism and art isn't always so smooth—and much of it is downright troubling.

The Spike Lee-Michael Jordan pairing began back in 1987—before the *Right Thing* script was even written—for two spots shown during a 1988 National Basketball Association all-star game. Spike, Mike and Nike proved a winning team and went on to produce further editions in the same lively, funny and visually clever series. In February 1989, several months before *Do the Right Thing*'s American release, Nike had begun airing TV commercials with Spike, Michael Jordan and his namesake shoes, Nike Air Jordans. The campaign and the shoes were both instant winners: Nike posted an incredible 48 percent sales increase on the basis of the Mars-Michael campaign.

The now-famous spots, shot in a grainy black-and-white reminiscent of *She's Gotta Have It*, had Spike reprising his Mars Blackmon role—something he said he'd never do. Mars does his patented nonstop-talking act, repeatedly repeating himself ("D'ya know, Professor? D'ya know? D'ya know?"). Wisely, the vertically challenged Spike leaves both the hoop work and the girl getting to Jordan. There's nothing inherently immoral or underhanded about Spike doing these commercials, even if most image-conscious American personalities of his stature avoid such endorsements (or, like Woody Allen, do them in Japan, where they think nobody's looking). But when he sticks that same product into his scripts, he slam dunks both ethics and artistic credibility.

On *Do the Right Thing*'s scorching Saturday, Buggin' Out has a confrontation with a Yuppie (played by John Savage in a Boston Celtics shirt—Spike Lee shorthand for Antichrist) who accidentally smudges Buggin' Out's gleaming white Air Jordans. In no time, this minor event has blown up into one of those idiotic street hassles urban dwellers must periodically face—the *homo sapiens* equivalent of rams locking horns. Ahmad and other teens from the 'hood back up Buggin' Out, echoing his taunts about how he ought to "fuck up" the white boy "*two* times" for this unforgivable crime against footwear. Every urban dweller knows that, in a racially charged climate, a situation like this can rapidly escalate from standard-issue street hassle to large-scale civil unrest (as Spike demonstrates as Radio Raheem is transformed first into Air Raheem and then into Dead Raheem in rapid succession).

As for Buggin' Out's sidewalk stand-off with the ponytailed Celtics traitor, it's worth noting that Spike originally considered taking the role not of Mookie, but of Buggin'. (This would have been a connection between star and shoes a little too cozy even for Spike.) As more than one writer has pointed out, the drenching of a (white-owned) car is presented as harmless tomfoolery, but a stain on a pair of (black-owned) running shoes practically sets off a righteous race riot. "Spike Lee apparently believes in two kinds of justice," carped a critic in London's *Empire* magazine. "One for the hip, and one for the square."

Yes, Spike is delivering the diversity and complexity he promises us as an artist—though not without an unsubtle slant and a certain measure of hypocrisy. To toss the audience a two-sided coin is every artist's prerogative. But a two-*headed* coin is another story. Consequently, there are times when *Right Thing* seems less like a work of political philosophy than a high-stakes poker game.

Speaking of sleight-of-hand, is it mere coincidence that Buggin' Out's bruised sneakers are clearly identified in the dialogue as Air Jordans?

In the industry, this is known as product placement: a common though not particularly respectable practice by which corporations pay to have their products mentioned and/or featured in movies. These days, the whores of Hollywood maneuver such commercial considerations with alarming regularity, but a self-proclaimed *auteur* like Spike is supposed to be above that sort of thing. (Scorsese avoids it, and hardliner Woody would sooner colorize.)

It was one thing for Spike to mention the Ferry Bank restaurant in the credits of *She's Gotta Have It*, or even the prominent Adidas logo's placement on *School Daze*'s G Phi G uniforms. Back in those days, Spike was a struggling indie filmmaker who needed to keep costs down any way he could. By his third film, he was dealing with millions and was no longer quite so desperate.

But product-placement concerns are only the beginning of the story. Soon after the commercials began airing, the other shoe dropped: the Air Jordan line was in such demand that teenagers began fighting and in some cases even killing each other over the flashy runners. In some sad, sick parody of one of Spike's own commercials, "Is it the shoes? Is it the shoes?" became a shout heard round the world.

New York Post sportswriter Phil Mushnick fired the first salvo, accusing Spike—but mostly athletes like Jordan and Bo Jackson—of a take-the-money-and-run philosophy by which they can peddle running shoes to ghetto customers who clearly have more important things to do with their limited resources. *Village Voice* sports journalist Allen Barra then joined the chorus, taking Spike to task for his seemingly nonchalant response to the tragedies: "The Nike commercials Michael Jordan and I do have never gotten anyone killed. . . . These kids feel they have no options, no opportunities. America tells everyone 'Buy, Buy, Buy,' it's capitalism at its Best/Worst, and folks who don't have want to 'get' by hook or by crook." On another occasion, with another journalist, Spike again bristled at the topic: "Shit, what about it? It's my fault, it's Michael Jordan's fault, that kids are buying these shoes? That's just the trigger. There's more to it than that." (For his part, Michael Jordan also pleaded innocent in *Sports Illustrated*. But at least he came out of the media storm looking better than Spike did after expressing deep sorrow for the incidents in a near-tears interview.)

Writer Walter Kirn opened the wound again in a bitter invective published in the August 1990 *GQ* magazine. "Although Lee credits his own success to a culture-filled home and a close, loving family, the Nike Air Jordan commercials he stars in and directs have a different message for youth: Be cool on the street, walk tall in the playground. This ethos isn't likely to produce Michael Jordans. At best, it may inspire a generation of flashy nightclub hangers-on." Kirn has some interesting pokes at Spike elsewhere in his diatribe, but here he is off the mark. Battles for schoolyard status date back to the beginning of public education; what's turned them toxic lately is the presence not of trainers, but of guns.

Spike explained his views to *Playboy*. "The value system of black youth is very distorted. There's too much emphasis on materialism—gold chains, cars, even sneakers. I know Nike is fronting this, but let's be honest. And this gold stuff is just crazy. We need a whole re-evaluation of our value system." But how is it that black teenagers' fetish of boom-boxes and gold chains represents "distorted values," but the fetish of $125 shoes does not? Could it have anything to do with who's doing the promoting?

The target audience that Spike is selling to looks at a pair of Nikes the way their Clifton, New Jersey, counterparts look at a Camaro Z28. These are (relatively) inexpensive status symbols for a crowd with very little status; more than shoes, they're signifiers. For ghetto kids, any status, however shallow or deceptive, is worth something. Like graffiti, it confirms their existence and proclaims, "Contrary to popular belief, I *exist!*"

Yes, kids have killed each other over Nikes—but they've also killed each other over jewelry, drugs, money, girlfriends and dirty looks. For once, Spike may have a point about Thinly Veiled Racism: to propose that he should refrain from promoting sneakers because black kids will murder for them implies that they are all essentially psychopaths, unable to discern that taking life over laces may not be a good thing. The vast majority of these kids legitimately buy these shoes with their own money and wear them without being hassled. These killings, though shameful, are aberrations—robberies gone mad. The sneakers could just as easily have been any other (perceived) valuable.

Mushnick and Barra make no mention of untimely death from drunk driving after drinking ballpark beer—let alone connect it to the jocks who flack for the breweries. But then, the fans who can actually afford today's major league ticket prices are mostly white, and if one ran over a pedestrian on the drive home from the stadium, chances are he would not be portrayed as a murderous cretin—as opposed to mindless, soulless black kids so doped up on crack and consumerism they'll start a shooting war over shoes. This attitude is, at best, patronizing and, at worst, racist.

Spike pushes a product that will make you hip in your peer group. Unlike the costlier power purchases of white America (cars, houses, Rolexes, psychotherapy), a black kid can usually scrape together enough green for a little Day-Glo leather and rubber for his feet—even at the high-profit-margin price of $125. That certain psychos within the community will kill for this is the fault neither of Spike Lee nor of his commercials. Instead, it's the conditions under which human beings are reduced and debased that should be put under the interrogation lamp.

Those who whine "It's society's fault" anytime something goes wrong are generally not to be trusted. But in this case, there are clearly larger social forces at play than Spike Lee. For these problems, Spike has never claimed to have the answers. To deny black heroes like Spike and Michael Jordan a piece of the capitalist pie is to impose on them a stricter moral code than we do on famous white players who've been raking it in from beer barons and shaving cream kingpins for decades.

Even so, Spike's quit-picking-on-me attitude leaves a bad taste in one's mouth. Even if he weren't directly responsible, he could still have sounded more sorry. Someone who plays the PR game as well as Spike Lee does should know that. The problem was less his promotion than his insensitive response—especially compared to Michael Jordan's heartfelt compassion—to the tragic results. It wouldn't have been so bad had Spike given *some* indication of his concern—a statement or contribution in support of the Stop The Violence anti-gang movement, for instance.

"Let's try to deal effectively with the conditions that make a kid put so much importance on a pair of sneakers," is Spike's defense. And it's a good one. Regarding what makes inner-city youth kill each other over trivialities, the question, "Is it the shoes?" can be safely answered *Hell, no!* Shoes are a symptom, not the disease. Charged with being an accessory to murder by promoting slick sneakers, there is no alternative but to find Spike Lee *not guilty*.

Also, in Spike's defense, he is extremely selective about what he will or will not do in the advertising arena. "I don't want to get into that world of commercials where ad-agency executives stand over your shoulder saying they don't like the color of blue or the way this cornflake is shaped." He has turned down far more requests to make commercials than he has accepted, and only takes the bait when he both approves of the product and feels he can do something creative with the medium. Whatever the outcome on the street, Spike's Nike commercials were entertaining and very cinematic examples of the contemporary commercial medium, and his Levi's 501 spots were also memorable.

But he also knows what to turn down. No sooner had *She's Gotta Have It* proven itself a hit than the California Wine Cooler people offered Spike $50,000 to have him do Mars. But Spike didn't want to be associated with an intoxicating beverage. For one thing, he is a very moderate drinker. But more important, he is among the prominent African-Americans who feel that alcohol companies, by targeting ghetto consumers, make the uplift of the race just that much more difficult. Particularly under fire have been the brewers of malt liquor (beer with 50% more alcohol for the same price as regular suds) who have recruited such celebrity spokespersons as Billy Dee Williams (for Colt 45) and Ice Cube (for St. Ides). (The St. Ides people have also felt the wrath of Public Enemy's Chuck D who, in leaflets reading "Chuck D Wants Witnesses" available at Spike's Joint, claims St. Ides illegally sampled his voice in their radio commercials. The flyers explain his case against the brewery and his general opposition to their product, and ask for those who heard the ads to support his crusade.)

Spike has also found time to pose for clothes *not* from his own films, such as for the Gap and for the gentlemen's clothier Barney's New York (for whom Spike topped a slick Italian suit, dress shirt, silk tie and diamond earring with his man-of-the-people baseball cap). Rather than pocket the money, Spike did the right thing and donated his $2,000 fee to the United Negro College Fund. "Plus," Spike added in his *Do the Right Thing* book, "the movie [*Do the Right Thing*] was coming out. I knew it it couldn't hurt."

Not all of Spike Lee's extracurricular activities are quite so mercenary. He also programs an annual series of seminars for entry-level minority filmmakers at Long Island University featuring lectures by himself, Ernest Dickerson, his props and costumes department heads, and others. And, in the midst of 1989's summer *Do the Right Thing* flare-up, he found the time to talk to 120 of the nation's best high school basketball players at Nike's annual basketball camp at Princeton. Spike (and Monty Ross) went to the college to share some life-skills advice to a group of young men, many of whom would soon be going on to big money in the National Basketball Association. "When I was a kid, I wanted to be a basketball player, but I stopped growing," he said, to much laughter. But when he declared, "I never smoked a joint in my life," they didn't laugh, but applauded.

In 1989, Spike also supervised *Do It A Cappella*, a one-hour television special of doo-wop and vocal-harmony groups, including Sweet Honey in the Rock and Ladysmith Black Mambazo. Although such a project for public television does not earn his company much in the way of cash dollars, it nonetheless brings him to wider audiences than he can lure to his movies.

One of Spike's many commercial ventures of the very busy year of 1989 didn't quite pan out—for reasons both bizarre and beyond his control. Folks in both the 40 Acres and the Public Enemy camps were hoping "Fight the Power" would be the band's first big AM hit, with the movie and the song cross-promoting each other in a way that always helps a movie do well at the box office.

"Fight the Power," *DTRT*'s theme song, was to be released as a single. The Public Enemy album *Fear of a Black Planet* contained a slightly different, radio-ready mix, in which Flavor Flav's notorious line about Elvis, "motherfuck him *and* John Wayne," was toned down to "motherBLEEP him and John Wayne." Although "Fight" was a rawer brand of rap than the airwaves usually tolerate, the objectionable language had been removed from the mix, and the song stood a decent chance as a single. What prevented this was the firing of a loose cannon called Professor Griff.

Right at the time of *Do the Right Thing*'s release, Public Enemy's "Minister of Information" Professor Griff made reckless and offensive statements to a reporter from the *Washington Times* concerning Jews' alleged responsibility "for most of the wickedness" in the world. The ensuing controversy killed whatever chance for crossover success that "Fight the Power" might have had. "Chuck did the right thing," felt Spike. Griff was talking not from facts but from bigotry and "had to go." (Griff has since recanted, saying he has been reading up on the Holocaust at the Nation of Islam resource center, and now regrets having trivialized the Jewish people's sufferings.)

Instead, Spike found a different way to extend the *Do the Right Thing*/Public Enemy connection: yet another remix was later issued on 12-inch single featuring an extended conversation between Spike and Public Enemy's Flavor Flav about (among other things) hypocritical entertainers who tell *Rolling Stone* things like, "Don't call me a black singer, I just want to be a singer who happens to be black"; actors who go on TV to preach "Just say no to drugs" while being high themselves; why George Michael was in the R&B

category on the American Music Awards; and, of course, the inevitable reference to blue contact lenses.

By this time, Spike Lee was not only fighting the power, he *was* the power.

Chapter 10

1989–90: *Mo' Better* Makes It Mo' Better

After *Do the Right Thing*—and all the fallout that followed—Spike Lee understandably felt the need for a change of pace. Not a retreat, and certainly not a surrender, but just something a little quieter and subtler.

Spike also wanted to demonstrate his versatility both as a writer and as a director. He felt the need to prove that he did not need constant controversy and confrontation to make his work interesting. He knew he was capable of doing more than just, in Eddie Murphy's words, "the militant brother stuff." Spike was wise to follow Mr. Señor Love Daddy's advice and just "Chill *out!*"

This did not mean that he wouldn't again explore dangerous areas like racism. "I didn't want to repeat myself right away," Spike explained. "There are a great many subject matters I want to tackle. I come from a jazz household. I had seen *Bird* and *Round Midnight*, and they gave me the impetus to do a film about jazz." And, he felt, "It was just a matter of time."

But Spike can only be Spike; he could not do just the same old jazz thing. Spike knew he wanted to avoid the dark, depressing and claustrophobic atmospheres of two recent, generally well-reviewed jazz movies from prominent (white) directors: Bertrand Tavernier's French production *Round Midnight*, and (especially) Clint Eastwood's Charlie Parker bio-pic *Bird*. Spike told his designer Wyn Thomas he didn't think *Mo' Better Blues* should look like *Bird*. "I don't think *anything* should look like *Bird*," quipped Thomas, who then set about creating the stylish set for the club where Bleek spends his evenings entertaining. Nor had Spike been particularly satisfied with earlier Hollywood looks at jazz, such as *St. Louis Blues* (1958) and *Paris Blues* (1962), which either saddled their black players with predictable addiction problems or relegated them to sidekick status.

Donald Bogle, author of *Blacks in American Film and Television*, summed up these frustrations well when he wrote, "Director Tavernier . . . has no idea how Blacks relate to one another, the type of humor and pull and tug that enlivens conversations, the connective cultural tissue (the set of references, the use of language, the body rhythms themselves) that would make these people feel so much at home with one another." This comment was made, remember, despite the presence of a real-life jazz legend Dexter Gordon, as the fictional Dale Turner in Tavernier's film.

What did all these earlier films have in common, other than jazz soundtracks? Despite black characters and music, they were all directed by Whites. Jazz is recognized the world over as the original African-

American music form, yet there was not one significant feature film on the subject by a black director. Clearly, Spike would have to do something about *that*.

As the first black director to make a jazz movie, Spike would be doing things a little differently. For one thing, Spike was disturbed that drugs and alcohol have figured so prominently in jazz movies in the past. "That's been the image of black people in general in films," he complained. "I have to point out that jazz musicians are not the only professional type that's not been truly represented on film in terms of black people."

For years, Spike had been collecting many terms for sex in his mind; among his all-time favorites had been "the mo' better." So Bleek Gilliam's motto would be, "The mo' better makes it mo' better." This became extremely handy when the late jazz genius John Coltrane's widow Alice Coltrane declined Spike's request to call his fourth feature *Love Supreme*, after Coltrane's landmark 1964 LP. (At first Spike had been thinking of the authentically jazzy but cumbersome *Variations on the Mo' Better Blues*, a title which would surely have cost the film untold millions in lost revenue.) Mrs. Coltrane did, however, grant Spike's more important wish: to use a section of her late husband's landmark album "A Love Supreme" on his film's soundtrack.

Branford Marsalis and Terence Blanchard, jazz heroes to a younger generation (and Coltrane worshipers), would provide the horn solos for the original material performed on-screen by Bleek's and Shadow's bands. Nigerian-British pop-soul songstress Sade had originally been Spike's choice for

Clark, but the cool crooner turned him down. Similarly Gregory Hines declined the role of the slippery Shadow Henderson, which instead went to rising star Wesley Snipes, who played it superbly. As with *Do the Right Thing*'s replacing of Robert De Niro with Danny Aiello, some of Spike Lee's "letdowns" have turned out supremely well.

One actor, however, came through just as planned. The up-and-coming actor and sex symbol Denzel Washington, fresh from the underrated *The Mighty Quinn* and his Best Supporting Actor Oscar for 1989's excellent *Glory* agreed to play Bleek. Washington, though not a musician, could still look convincing on stage with a horn, and it didn't hurt that women responded to Washington the way they had to Billy Dee Williams fifteen or twenty years earlier.

But despite their good working relationship and their off-screen friendship, Spike still couldn't persuade Washington to take off his T-shirt for the love scene—nor was he impressed by having to appear in bed at all. "Spike, I can't be doing this stuff," Washington implored. "I've got a wife and two sons." Spike said he supposed he understood, but wished Washington had told him that before. Audiences seemed to find the star attractive enough even with a shirt.

Another disappointment—though by now a familiar one—was in the accounting department. As usual, Spike was asking the studio (this time Universal) for mo' money than they were willing to put up. Spike said he needed $11.5 million, but settled for $10 million. This is, by current standards, still very modest, and Spike is correct in saying that part of the reason Hollywood tolerates him is that he can make good, popular pictures more economically than his free-spending competition in the old guard.

The movie was shot in Brooklyn (near the Brooklyn Bridge and in Prospect Park), in midtown Manhattan, and on a soundstage in Queens, from September 24 through December 1, 1989. At ten weeks, the shoot took two weeks longer than either *School Daze* or *Do the Right Thing*, making it Spike's longest to date.

Where his sister Joie was concerned, it was also the most fractious and unhappy. The siblings clashed as Spike and his father had done over Dad's plans for a jazz theme for Mars Blackmon in *She's Gotta Have It*. Joie Lee had questions about her character's motivation that she didn't feel her brother was answering adequately.

Meanwhile, Spike gathered other members of the old gang for the crowd. The astute can catch glimpses of *She's Gotta Have It*'s Tracy Camilla Johns and Tommy Hicks, as well as one-time Kid Creole and the Coconuts sidekick Coati Mundi. For one member of Spike Lee's emerging stock company, however, *Mo' Better Blues* would be his final appearance.

Everyone at 40 Acres and a Mule was shocked and saddened when Robin Harris died quietly in his sleep in the March following wrap. Shooting was over, so Harris's death didn't affect the film itself, but the comic's passing at age thirty-six was still a blow to Spike. The heavyset comedian, a big star in black comedy circles, had stolen scenes in *Do the Right Thing* as "corner man" Sweet Dick Willie. In *Mo'*

Better Blues, Harris is memorable as Butterbean, the pink-suited comic who entertains at Beneath the Underdog between Bleek's sets. Spike was understandably shaken by the funnyman's death: apart from anything else, Harris was only three years older than Spike. Spike gave Robin Harris a special tribute both on celluloid and on paper: "Robin Hughes Harris, in loving memory, Aug. 30, 1953–Mar. 18, 1990."

By May, however, it was back to business as usual for Spike, as he pulled another of those stunts that keep gossip columnists gossiping. At the Coro Foundation's "Commitment to Leadership Dinner," a high-profile charity event held annually in New York, Spike set off yet another media storm while sharing the stage with journalist-novelist Tom Wolfe. Perhaps knowing Wolfe's penchant for blinding ice-cream suits, Spike turned up in tasteful black.

Most of the evening was pleasant, even to the point of being slightly dull. Trust Spike Lee to liven things up a little. Having got a hold of the shooting script of the $45 million film version of Wolfe's best-selling novel, *The Bonfire of the Vanities*, Spike revealed to Wolfe—and to the world—that the ending of the book had been radically altered for the screen. Director Brian de Palma (*The Untouchables*, *Dressed to Kill*), Spike announced, had changed Wolfe's climax so that the black youth Charles Lamb, who was injured by financier-socialite Sherman McCoy's car, yanks off his life-support system and walks out of the hospital. Since this would imply that Lamb had exaggerated his injuries for publicity purposes, it distorted the entire point of the story.

The assembled diners were more shocked by this revelation than was the novelist himself, who was strangely unconcerned by it. He insisted that, as a novelist, his job was done. The filming of his work interested him so little he hadn't even witnessed any of the shooting.

Spike was stunned—and vicariously indignant. "You write a great book," he blurted, "and you don't care what they do with it? You just take the money and run? I can't believe you haven't read the script or been to the set." Wolfe simply reasserted that he trusted the people involved to do a good job. To Spike, who has never known the luxury of being able to leave everything to others, this was an alien concept. Spike is known for controlling every detail of his films right down to the lobby cards: he came up in the film industry the hard way and is used to a hands-on approach.

Tom Wolfe might not have cared, but the people making *Vanities* did. Director de Palma denounced Spike, advising him to "concentrate on making better movies instead of pontificating." Considering that this is the man who made *Wise Guys* and *Casualties of War*—and that *Bonfire of the Vanities* was about to become the most notorious disaster since *Heaven's Gate*—de Palma was in no position to be telling Spike Lee about "making better movies." Some of Spike's pictures have been seriously flawed, but de Palma has let off upwards of half a dozen stink bombs.

Lucy Fisher, Warner Brothers' executive in charge of production on *Vanities*, called Spike the next morning to give him hell for leaking this confidential information. Fisher's point was that if the director wanted to play in the big leagues and make movies with Hollywood money, he had to obey certain rules. Among the most sacred of those rules is no one—not even film critics—should ever give away a movie's ending. Spike defended himself as best he could, though he realized that, this time, he had done the wrong thing. Consequently, he restrained himself from retaliating with his customary thunder. Not only was Fisher a major executive, but she was at Warner Brothers—which just happened to be the studio that owned the rights to *The Autobiography of Malcolm X*.

Fisher, for her part, also toned down her criticism more than she might have liked to have done. After all, however much trouble Spike Lee might cause, his movies still make money—and some day, the Brothers Warner might want one of them to make money for *them*. Spike and Fisher each recognized that the other was too important to burn all bridges.

Interestingly, Spike's *Vanities* bonfire made no difference to the film's eventual reception. In its brief Christmas 1990 release, the movie was delivered to theaters DOA. Due less to the altered ending than to idiotic casting, *Vanities* suffered reviews of almost unprecedented hostility and lost tens of millions of dollars. And within a year, Spike would indeed be making a movie with Warner money: the long-awaited *Malcolm X*.

In July, Spike was approached to sign a petition demanding that the Classification and Ratings Administration (CARA) branch of the MPAA update its antiquated ratings system. Specifically, the call was for a more modern replacement for the "X." People in the industry wanting the change knew what Spike had been through over the "X" the MPAA had wanted to give _She's Gotta Have It_. So with other prominent directors such as Jonathan Demme (_Silence of the Lambs_) and Pedro Almodovar (_Tie Me Up! Tie Me Down!_), Spike signed the petition to have the tainted X-rating replaced with an A (Adult) or M (Mature) category instead. Later that year, CARA finally relented and instigated the NC-17 (No children at all under 17). This was welcomed by the industry as a victory for artistic freedom—though one that arrived too late to help _She's Gotta Have It_, which would not have needed cutting had the NC-17 category been in place in 1986.

For October, Spike accepted Bob Guccione, Jr.'s offer of "full control" to guest-edit an issue of his pop-music magazine, _SPIN_. "I was only vaguely familiar with _SPIN_ magazine," Spike wrote in his opening editorial. "I had seen it around and on occasion would pick up a copy to read; no more, no less." Despite admitting his lack of familiarity with the publication, Spike nonetheless _knew_ that he had done a better job than the magazine's usual staff. In his own humble opinion, Spike's _SPIN_ was not only "the Blackest issue they've ever had," but "I might add, it may be one of their best."

Having included that obligatory bit of self-congratulation, Spike then launched into an interesting but essentially irrelevant tirade against the U.S. corporations who still were trading with South Africa. Singled out for special scorn was Citibank, with whom

Spike announced he had closed all his accounts. Only a year later, Spike himself would be doing business with South Africa—the country that had imprisoned his friend Nelson Mandela for twenty-six years—when the director insisted on shooting scenes for *Malcolm X* in Soweto.

One of the more memorable features of Spike's *SPIN* issue was the frank rap session he held with his buddy (and occasional sparring partner) Eddie Murphy. Spike again prodded Murphy to use his clout as Paramount's biggest moneymaker to bring more Blacks into the studio. The two men had been through this one before; again, Murphy countered that he was doing as much as he could, and that it wasn't as simple as Spike made it out to be. The battle ended, as it always does, in a stalemate, with Spike insistent that Murphy could do more, and Murphy equally insistent that he couldn't.

The familial feeling of the issue even extended to a feature on Joie Lee and her supporting role in 1990's Matt Dillon-Sean Young gobbler *A Kiss Before Dying* (her only significant part to date outside of her brother's *oeuvre*). The quality of the rest of the issue varied wildly, ranging from an eloquent and moving essay on bringing black stories to the screen by playwright August Wilson (*Fences, Two Trains Running*) to a comparatively moderate and reasonable talk with celebrity preacher Al Sharpton.

For the youngbloods, there was also Public Enemy's Chuck D and his self-styled "media assassin" Harry Allen on a barely coherent tirade against blue-eyed devils. Rappers may be able to get away with sweeping generalizations and inflammatory revisionism on a three-minute dance track, but national magazines are supposed to deal in data and history, not outrage and hearsay.

Shortly thereafter, *SPY* magazine ran a tally of the number of times Spike had mentioned himself, his movies or his family in that issue of *SPIN*:

> Number of times Spike Lee's name is mentioned: 43
>
> Number of times Joie Lee's name is mentioned: 16
>
> Number of times *Mo' Better Blues* is mentioned: 12
>
> Number of visual representations of Spike Lee: 8

And so on. No wonder Spike thinks it's one of their best issues ever: it's devoted almost entirely to him!

But then, hogging the limelight is nothing new to Spike. The *School Daze* book was the first of the "companion volumes" Spike created in collaboration with *Village Voice* writer (and close friend) Lisa Jones. Of the three books on which the pair has collaborated, it's worth noting that Jones gets credit on the books' covers but *not* on their spines: when placed on a shelf, only one of the two names can be seen.

That name is not Lisa Jones.

Chapter 11

1990: The Spike Quintet: Five Guys Named *Mo'*

"Yo, Spike, start the movie!" cackles Public Enemy's Flavor Flav over the Universal Pictures logo as *Mo' Better Blues* lurches into Act One.

Once again, we are attending a Spike Lee Joint, produced, written and directed by Spike Lee. Opening titles inform us we are in Brooklyn, New York, 1969. Running up to a window on a tree-lined residential street, a group of boisterous boys shout for young Bleek Gilliam to come out to play. In the Gilliam family's spacious, tasteful brownstone, ten-year-old Bleek complains about having to practice his trumpet when he'd much rather play ball with his friends.

Cut to: same lips, same trumpet, twenty years later. We must assume Bleek has been doing his practicing, because he's now the leader of a jazz ensemble that not only bears his name, but works steadily. Bleek's rival in his own band, Shadow Henderson (Wesley Snipes), is taking prolonged solos, foreshadowing future friction. The band's manager, Giant (Spike Lee), reminds Bleek that it's his, Bleek's band, and he should restrain Shadow's grandstanding. On the sidelines are Left Hand Lacey (Giancarlo Esposito looking like Kid Creole), Bottom Hammer (Bill Nunn), and Rhythm (Jeff "Tain" Watts). Together, they comprise The Bleek Quintet. Apart, they are five very different African-American musicians on a big roll. Night after night, they pack their fashionable club, a venue decidedly more upscale than the name Beneath the Underdog (which Spike borrowed from the autobiography of jazz great Charles Mingus) would suggest.

But music is less the focus here than Bleek's private life. The poor lad is suffering from too much affection from too many women. Both Clark (the lovely newcomer Cynda Williams) and Indigo (Joie Lee) make demands on his time. Bleek's female trouble is complicated by Clark's wanting to sing with the band; Bleek insists she's not professional enough. His rival Shadow, however, is more than willing to give her a go. In turn, each of his two women informs Bleek that he doesn't know what he wants: telling rather than showing, breaking basic storytelling sense again. Bleek also gets grief from Giant, who not only can't get the group a raise but is losing big to a bookie named Petey (actor-salsa star Ruben Blades).

Spike freely admits the gambling subplot was inspired by baseball's Pete Rose scandal (the

player-manager convicted of betting on major-
league games with which he was involved). "Giant's
idol is Pete Rose," Spike said in the *Mo' Better*
book, efficiently tagging his character as a loser.
Giant's gambling problem has gotten to the point
where a couple of thugs named Madlock (Samuel L.
Jackson) and Rod (Leonard Thomas) are sent to give
Giant a lesson about the prompt payment of debts.
The enforcers fling open their car door just as Giant
is passing on his bike, throwing him off the saddle
and onto the pavement. The hoods then take Giant
for a little ride and explain how they don't believe
in killing their brothers and sisters, only in caus-
ing them severe and lasting pain. They then
break Giant's hand as a warning of worse things
to come.

Meanwhile Giant is trying to obtain a better
deal for the band from club owners Moe and
Josh Flatbush. They counter that he's trying to
take the food out of their children's mouths (yes,
they actually say that) and that the contract is not up
for renegotiation. Things go from bad to worse for
Giant when, fingers still bandaged from his previous
lesson in street economics, he gets hauled out of
the men's room and into the alley by Madlock and
Rod. There, they start giving their half-pint victim
a ferocious beating.

When Bleek finally hears the racket over the
noise of the band, he comes to Giant's defense.
For his troubles, Bleek gets smacked in the mouth
with his own horn, damaging his precious lips and
ruining his career in the space of two bars. Both
Bleek and Giant suffer savagely, but only Bleek's
career will be ruined because of it.

After a year of surgery and introspection, Bleek gets the idea that Indigo was really the girl for him after all—especially after he's seen Clark singing (very nicely, thank you) for the new Shadow Henderson Quartet. Spike tries to compress the next several years of Bleek's life (marriage to Indigo, the birth of their child) into a seven-and-three-quarter minute montage set to Coltrane's "Acknowledgement," the opening passage from *A Love Supreme*. Most critics, however much they may have liked the preceding two hours (or Coltrane's music), found this prolonged wrap-up unconvincing and an artistic misjudgment.

Worse, Spike seems confused about what *kind* of supreme love Coltrane was addressing: as used in the film to score Bleek and Indigo's whirlwind romance, marriage and parenthood, it is the earthly love of the bed. As indicated clearly in Coltrane's own liner notes, "A Love Supreme" is about love of God—a kind of love nowhere addressed in *Mo' Better Blues*.

Throughout most of the film, Bleek tries to keep both Clark and Indigo at arm's length so he can devote himself to his craft. It was with these thin strands of plot that Spike has weaved a story that winds on for 127 minutes—his longest film to date, and a bit of a grind for most viewers.

Admittedly, *Mo' Better Blues* is a wonderful movie to look at, full of stylish clothes and fixtures that somehow manage to look like the 1940s and the 1990s at the same time. Spike even wears a tie, an item of clothing he normally eschews for his designer-homeboy duds. (Costume credit goes, as usual, to Ruth E. Carter.) The film's visual opulence was even reflected in its seductively colorful ad campaign, featuring Spike-as-Giant touting a wallful of posters of Denzel Washington, Joie Lee and Cynda Williams against a brick wall. Just behind the *Mo' Better* posters are plastered-over *Do the Right Thing* ads—another of Spike's little self-referential (or perhaps self-*reverential*) touches.

Musicians have remarked on the wonderful authenticity Spike captured in the dressing room scenes, which seem almost like a documentary in their easy-going naturalism. *Mo' Better* might not correct all the mistakes of jazz movies of the past, but for the effortless *blackness* of offstage interplay, Spike can genuinely congratulate himself. The trouble is that, having established a convincing setting, the drama that should be taking place there is sometimes lacking.

In *School Daze*, the spiky Spike slipped the dean a couple of lines chiding his race for their lackluster record on funding Negro colleges. This is a failing, his script notes, not common among other minorities. *Mo' Better Blues* has his trumpeter hero chastising Blacks at a jazz club for being less enthusiastic supporters of the original African-American musical form than Whites. It has been noticed, however, that despite Bleek's speech, most of the extras with which the director has populated his set are Black—which tends to undermine his own argument. Once again, Spike wanted it both ways: he couldn't resist giving acting work to his black applicants, thus creating a false ring to Bleek's complaint that "our people" don't support jazz.

Although nobody asked, that didn't stop Spike from writing, "OK, OK, I know you're wondering if this Bleek character is Spike. All I can say is I love film more than Bleek loves his music." Perhaps *Mo' Better*'s fatal flaw is that Spike cares about this question far more than any audience could be expected to. Others thought that Bleek and Shadow might be fictionalized versions of brothers Wynton and Branford Marsalis. Trumpeter Terence Blanchard thinks otherwise. In a 1990 magazine interview he said, "A lot of people asked me if it was depicting the Marsalis brothers, but I didn't get that sense at all. When I first met Denzel Washington we were in a car with Spike Lee driving to Atlantic City to see Mike Tyson. Denzel and I began talking about different aspects of his character. . . . It didn't occur to me until later but, more than any one person, Denzel's character Bleek Gilliam was really Spike Lee. His struggle as an artist, his relationship with women—it's all there."

But Spike's resemblance to Bleek is not nearly so strong as his resemblance to Giant. Psychologists call this transference: unconscious attributing of one's own characteristics to another. "Being loud is probably his way of compensating for being small in stature. Though it's never mentioned in the dialogue, no one gave him the nickname Giant; he gave it to himself." This is indeed revealing— not about Giant, but about Spike.

In June of 1990, *Mo' Better Blues* was released to mixed reviews but fairly decent box-office success for its $10 million investment. Again, no Academy Awards were forthcoming, but Wynton and Branford Marsalis did get a Grammy nomination for the soundtrack album.

Spike's superb instincts—his nose for what works cinematically—have helped him through rough patches before, though never more than in *Mo' Better Blues*. This script, applied to the screen by someone without Spike Lee's abilities to make the dull seem interesting, would be sleep-inducing at best. Reel after reel unspools with characters unchanged and the story no further ahead: Bleek likes one girl; Bleek likes the other girl; or maybe Bleek just likes to play his horn; or maybe he likes the first girl best after all. Pass the hot-buttered No-Doz.

Of course, no Spike Lee movie is complete without controversy—even one that was supposed to be just a change of pace. "I must be careful to avoid stereotypes," Spike wrote in his notes for *Right Thing*. At the time, he was concerned about his portrayal of Italian-Americans. The Italians took it pretty well—especially considering their community leaders had previously raised concerns about their depiction in the *Godfather* series and other mafia movies. Spike's trouble came not in 1989 and not from Italians, but about a year later, with an entirely different minority.

If only he had heeded his own advice about stereotyping when creating the characters of Moe and Josh Flatbush, *Mo' Better*'s Jewish club owners. As played by real-life brothers John and Nicholas Turturro, Moe and Josh Flatbush are nothing if not memorable. Spike's portrayal of sheckel-grubbing shysters who live only to chisel black artists out of what is rightfully theirs is like something out of a Klan comic book. Although the Flatbushes are precisely this kind of "negative" portrayal, Spike's worst crime was not outright hate-mongering but merely gross insensitivity. Offensive, yes, but not unforgivable.

What made the situation worse—at a time when relations between Blacks and Jews in New York City were at perhaps an all-time low thanks to a dirty mayoralty race—were Spike's hysterical denials. In what turned out to be a controversy almost as divisive as the race-riot questions about *Do the Right Thing*, Spike was accused of anti-semitism for his portrayal of the unmistakably Jewish Moe and Josh as the smiling, socially sanctioned con artists who run Beneath the Underdog. Moe and Josh have few scenes, but those contain only their gross attempts to swindle their musicians. In one, the two men do nothing but take turns praising the reliability of numbers against the unreliability of (presumably black) human beings. The brothers Flatbush are almost unbelievably clumsy caricatures—not just callous, but also so badly written as to be unworthy of their creator. Spike could hardly have been surprised when critics—both Jewish and gentile—called him on it.

Spike's defenses—in the *New York Times*, in his own companion book *Five for Five* and elsewhere—are among the weakest, least convincing things he has ever written. In the August 22, 1990 *New York Times*, Spike defended himself with "I Am Not an Anti-Semite," an unconvincing *mea culpa* delivered with the sledgehammer subtlety of its tell-all title. "What I try to do with all my characters is [to] offer what I feel are honest portraits of individuals with both faults and endearing characteristics." What, precisely, are the exploitive

Flatbush brothers' "endearing characteristics"? The two men are on-screen for, by Spike's estimate, ten minutes. During that time, they praise money and repeatedly try to chisel Bleek, his manager, and his band. That's it. What do we learn about their positive attributes, about their family lives or their individual complexities? Absolutely nothing. There is not a charming or endearing thing about either of them—culminating in their demand that Bleek get back on stage while he and Giant lie bleeding in the alley.

Spike constantly demands to know why he is expected to conform to a utopian pan-humanism when "the white boys" regularly get away with insulting minorities. It's a legitimate question, and Spike *is* scrutinized rather more closely than his pale-faced peers. But he can't have it both ways. Why is it that when other films offer "negative" role models for Blacks, they are seen to reflect America's pervasive white-supremacist power structure, but when Spike draws hideous stick figures like Moe and Josh, he claims them as merely "artistic creations" and therefore not representative of a wider contempt? What is the difference between a grade-Z shlockmeister caricaturing Blacks as pimps/pushers/whores, and Spike Lee caricaturing Jews as double-breasted, double-talking swindlers?

Are Moe and Josh "only characters"? Hardly. "All Jewish club owners are not like this, that's true, but these two are," Spike feebly wrote in the *New York Times*. But these are the only two Jewish club owners we see in *Mo' Better Blues*. If there are other kinds of Jewish club owners out there, we're certainly not seeing them in Spike's movies (nor has anybody forgotten that the Jews were the only group not allowed to respond during *Do The Right Thing*'s racial-slur sequence).

Further evidence of his bankruptcy as a debater was Spike's desperate invocation of Walt Disney's animated *Jungle Book* as a defense of his *Mo' Better* smear campaign. Crying "double standard," Spike sought to exonerate his own petty bigotries by attempting to taint Disney with the same. "Where were these articles [complaining of racial stereotypes] when Disney re-released *Jungle Book* this summer? Not a word, not a peep. Again, the double standard."

If indeed a double standard is at work here—and Spike will need to come up with a more salient example than the innocent *Jungle Book* if there is—it is a double standard that Spike is quite willing to apply himself when it's to his advantage. In what possible way can *Jungle Book* be construed as damaging to Blacks? Because it shows them in a jungle? Because Mowgli has a close rapport with nature? Because the book's author, Rudyard Kipling, was identified with British imperialism? Spike doesn't say: he's decided that *Jungle Book* is racist, and that's that.

"If critics are telling me that to avoid charges of anti-Semitism," he went on, spindly legs back-pedalling furiously, "all Jewish characters I write have to be model citizens, and not one can be a villain, cheat or a crook, and that no Jewish people have ever exploited black artists in the history of the entertainment industry, that's unrealistic and unfair." (This, by the way, rambles on for fifty-three barely coherent words—a run-on sentence of a sloppiness the *Times* would simply not tolerate from any writer who didn't happen to be a famous black film director.) That certainly *would* be unrealistic and unfair—but no one has ever suggested that. All that has been asked of Spike is that he show the kind of respect for other minority groups in his films that he's constantly and monotonously demanding for Blacks in white films. That is all any of his *Mo' Better* critics have ever called for.

In the same interview, he does make one good point, however, when he indicts the white journalists who predicted that life would imitate art in riotous ways as a result of the previous summer's *Do the Right Thing*. "Not a single one has had the honesty or integrity to admit their disservice to the film." After scoring one solid point, however, Spike immediately returned to his unfortunate habit of using the worst of the opposing side to justify his own failings. "What high moral ground are my critics writing from?" he asked rhetorically. The questions he should have been posing were, "Do I want to be as bad as they are?" and "Do their wrongs excuse mine?"

Throughout this latest crisis, we see Spike at his least attractive: the bullying, belligerent and illogical sides of his character that he occasionally can't control. Weak arguments, double standards, dirty fighting, sinking to the degraded level of his enemies—none of these tactics is beneath his pride when he feels cornered. "I'm an artist and I stand behind all my work, including my characters Moe and Josh Flatbush. As of now," Spike declared in the *Times* interview, "this matter is closed for me." Spike has spoken: having found himself not guilty, he dismisses the court. He's had the last word, so everyone should just let it drop.

But it would not go away, especially with Spike continuing to make statements he must have known would be offensive to others. "We [Blacks] produce the greatest artists in the world," Spike told the *Washington Post* in 1989. "Black people are the most creative people on earth," wrote Spike in his *Mo' Better Blues* book in 1990. These statements are not only patently absurd, they would have been attacked—probably by Spike Lee—had they been made by someone of another ethnic group. If a German were to say this about his people, he'd be branded a Nazi. If a Frenchman said it, he'd be attacked as an imperialist. But when Spike Lee says it about Blacks, it's accepted uncritically.

For *any* race to claim for itself the greatest creativity, spirituality or intelligence, is not only arrogant but stupid. Exactly how does one demonstrate such an assertion? Spike Lee can't prove that Blacks are the most creative any more than televangelists can prove only born-again Christians will get to heaven. Jews can't prove they're "the chosen people" and Nazis can't prove Aryans are "the master race." To make any of these claims is to deal not in fact but in opinions—and extremely silly, bigoted opinions at that.

Far from being continuously persecuted, however, there are instances where the media has actually been excessively kind and accepting of Spike's belligerent outbursts. In a 1991 *Playboy* interview, for instance, Spike was allowed to get away with the transparently false assertion that the United States waged war on Iraq because it is a nonwhite country, and that all of America's wars are against people of color. This is just about as ludicrous a claim as he has ever made, considering Iraq's population is no more or less "colored" than America's Gulf War allies in Kuwait and Saudi Arabia. Also, for the past forty years, Washington had no greater enemy than the (literally) Caucasian people of Russia. No one, however, called him on it.

If this is what happens when Spike Lee wants to make a quieter film, perhaps we should be glad he didn't try to make a bang.

Chapter 12

1990–91:
Spike of Bensonhurst

*The disturbing part about [getting caught by
a prison guard with a white pinup] was that
a terrible feeling of guilt came over me as I
realized that I had chosen the picture of the
white girl over the available pictures of black
girls. I tried to rationalize it away, but I was
fascinated by the truth involved. Why hadn't I
thought about it in this light before? So I took
hold of the question and began to inquire into
my feelings. Was it true, did I really prefer
white girls over black? The conclusion was
clear and inescapable: I did.*

—ELDRIDGE CLEAVER,
Soul on Ice (1970)

In notes for *Do the Right Thing* in 1988, Spike Lee
mentioned "having second thoughts about having

one of Sal's sons like Mookie's sister. It was done in *Mean Streets* and reminds me too much of Romeo and Juliet and all that forbidden love stuff." Like the subject of drugs, the interracial taboo was something he did get around to eventually. Also like the drug issue, the film Spike got around to it in was his 1991 release, *Jungle Fever*.

Spike's latest examination of racial attitudes was to be a bold and uncompromising dissection of the contemporary color bar as it applies to sex. The film's success or failure in the marketplace could only serve to divide feelings about the filmmaker even more sharply than before: his supporters would support him more than ever; his detractors would detract more than ever. But at least they could no longer accuse him of avoiding the crack question.

Village Voice writer and longtime Spike Lee confidant Nelson George has called the mass marketing of crack, beginning around 1986, "probably the decade's most important social event," one that would transform "first the American drug business and ultimately American life." Indeed, few people seem to realize just how much more dangerous the world became after the seemingly inconsequential shift from snorting to smoking cocaine. Purified through heating ("freebasing"), the innocent-looking white powder becomes both more intoxicating and more addictive, eliciting in the user a shorter, sharper high that even the strongest wills find difficult to resist.

"You don't have to be a racist to realize that leaving out the crack dealers in a film about Brooklyn's lower depths is like leaving out the hookers in a film about Times Square," wrote Walter Kirn in *GQ* about *Do the Right Thing*. As mentioned earlier, there were legitimate reasons for Spike skipping drugs in *Right Thing*—after all, there's only so much that can be crammed into one movie—so long as he made good on his promise to address it soon. With *Jungle Fever*, Spike wrote one of the most affecting portraits of an addicted personality—and, more important, of an entire addicted generation—ever put on the screen.

The filmmaker first touched on the topic of miscegenation in *Do the Right Thing*, when Sal flirted with Mookie's sister. And Mookie himself had Tina, his Puerto Rican girlfriend and mother of the mixed-blood baby Hector. Then, in *Mo' Better Blues*, Left Hand's Parisian girlfriend, Jeanne, excited comment in the dressing room and accused Giant of *racisme*. But these were just subplots, afterthoughts and inkspots compared to what Spike would do with *Jungle Fever*. This time he'd break the old taboo of black man and white woman.

First, though, he'd have to make it through the filming. The summer of 1990 blazed away as the director dug deep into enemy territory: the blue-collar Italian-American section of Brooklyn known as Bensonhurst. Bensonhurst was Spike's pick out of all the sections of New York: the Yusef Hawkins incident the previous summer at the time of *Do the Right Thing* was still fresh in everybody's mind. The neighborhood was known as a place where Blacks couldn't go—a reputation that someone of Spike Lee's temperament couldn't wait to challenge.

Up in Harlem, where he was also shooting scenes, Spike again engaged members of the Fruit of Islam for set security as he'd done with *Do the Right Thing*.

And again, he also hired a local crack addict to help out and to act as a consultant for authenticity on smoking rituals and other drug culture practices.

"When you're not shooting a film, you forget how fucking hard it is," Spike reported in the *Do the Right Thing* book. "Making films has got to be one of the hardest endeavors known to humankind. Straight up and down, film work is hard as shit." This time, it was going to be just a little harder, for reasons no one could foresee.

"COPS GUARD SPIKE LEE" screamed the front page of the New York *Daily News*. The *Jungle Fever* set in Bensonhurst had received death threats from persons unknown. Their sets had been defaced with racist graffiti. Someone had thrown a rock at Spike and Wesley Snipes. Production had reported the damage to the police, who then began providing protection for the film's main man. Just as Malcolm X had once been under police protection after his home in Queens had been firebombed in 1964, Spike was now being guarded by people he'd publicly dissed. The unsettling implication of the vandalism was that Spike Lee was simply not wanted in the neighborhood—that he was, in the Yusef Hawkins tradition, an unwelcome intruder up to no good. Also in the Hawkins tradition, he had broken no laws and done nothing wrong.

But *Jungle Fever* was not a smooth shoot for reasons well beyond the hostile environment in which he'd chosen to work. Spike clashed with leading lady Annabella Sciorra (later to be seen in *The Hand that Rocks the Cradle*) almost from the beginning. The on-set squabbles were the worst he'd ever had, making the differences of opinion with his sister Joie

over *Mo' Better Blues* seem like simple sibling rivalry. (Interestingly, this was the first time there would
be a Spike Lee movie with no part for Joie.)

Where Spike and Sciorra differed was over the
interpretation of her character: exactly *why* did
Angela Tucci, an Italian-American temporary secretary, rush into a brief but tumultuous affair with
her married African-American boss Flipper Purify
(Wesley Snipes)? Sciorra saw Angie as having
genuine feelings for Flipper; Spike wanted only
to emphasize the sexual curiosity factor. Sciorra,
according to costar Snipes, felt her character was
motivated by love, not lust. Both Spike and Snipes
felt the actress undervalued the importance of that
"fear of the big black dick" which Spike had spoken
of in interviews (and had even plastered all over early promotional materials for the film).

Having played a similar (though less likable)
character in 1989's *True Love*, Sciorra had some
familiarity with women like Angie—perhaps more
than Spike, whose firsthand knowledge of Italian-
American women has been limited and far from
intimate. So just maybe this young actress knew
what she was talking about. At any rate, she didn't
buy the essential hollowness of Spike's explanation.

Spike and Sciorra would look at the same words
in the script every morning, yet take away two
entirely different ideas of what they were supposed
to mean. As both writer and director, Spike had the
final say in the matter: he had the power to make
her say his words. But he could not control the *way*
Sciorra delivered those lines, or how he she held her
head or set her facial muscles. Through this subtle
subversion, Sciorra got her way.

To complicate matters, Flipper and Angie were a pair of lovers separated not just by complexion, but also by social status. Flipper, as a professional, clearly claimed a higher social standing than Angie, a secretary—and a temporary one to boot. So even if Angie didn't actually *love* Flip as Sciorra insisted, there was still ambition as a possible explanation for her attraction: as a lowly temp, hooking up with an architect would be a big step up in the world for her. By making Angie Tucci an interesting, complex character, Spike had inadvertently subverted his own plan to reduce everything to simplistic sexual gamesmanship. Strangely, Spike's script actually had more resonance and subtlety than he himself was giving it credit for—and only Annabella Sciorra saw it.

Today, Sciorra declines to speak about *Jungle Fever*. But critics were sympathetic to what she did with what she was given. Over the centuries, more compelling drama has been spun from love than from lust. If her Angie had really only wanted *it*, would she have taken as much abuse from her friends and family as she did? People in love go to extraordinary lengths to be together; people in lust either get their itch scratched or start looking elsewhere. If curiosity were really all that Angie and Flip had going for them, Spike could have ended the movie as soon as they'd had it off on Flip's drafting table.

In light of the ferocity of their clashes, Spike is surprisingly diplomatic when Sciorra's name comes up. "We didn't get along that great," Spike confessed to *Empire* magazine. "And now we don't talk" is his present position. But the filmmaker knew, personal feelings aside, that Sciorra "was the best person we auditioned. And," he hastens to add, "I must say, I think her performance is great." But his final (under)statement on the subject is, "Let's just say Annabella is hard to work with."

In addition to Sciorra and Snipes, Spike assembled his best cast yet: Ossie Davis and Ruby Dee would play the Good Reverend Doctor and his wife Lucinda. The ever-reliable John Turturro (almost unrecognizable in a kinky perm) would be the mild-mannered Paulie, Angie's old boyfriend and the only white character in Bensonhurst who has a good word to say about black people. The veteran Anthony Quinn would turn up in a cameo as Paulie's demanding dad. Frank Vincent from *Do the Right Thing* would return as Angie's bigoted father, and Samuel L. Jackson would graduate from walk-ons like Mister Señor Love Daddy and *Mo' Better Blues*'s Madlock to a role of substance: Gator, Snipes's ne'er-do-well older brother.

Almost as interesting as what went into the film is what was left out. Spike wrote a number of scenes between his character Cyrus and his real-life girlfriend, the model Veronica Webb, that didn't make the final cut, not because her acting wasn't good but because their moments *à deux* didn't advance the story and the film was already running long. Also deleted from the finished film was a tense confrontation in Manhattan between Flipper and the Bensonhurst gang. Flipper and Cyrus hear that Bensonhurst's defenders of white virginity are on their way to the two-tone couple's West Village love nest, intent on doing some harm. Flipper and Cyrus arm themselves with (you guessed it) Louisville Sluggers and go out to the street to meet the Neanderthals face to face. On the sidewalk, Cyrus recruits a couple of muscular gay Village residents by telling them a carload of suburban queer-bashers are on the way. Together, the four African-American men—two hetero, two homo— stand firm on the street and scare off the yahoos.

Another significant deletion was to have rounded off the Paulie-Orin subplot rather than leaving it hanging at Orin's front door as it was in the final version. Once inside, it turns out that Paulie has not actually arranged his date with Orin, but has just taken a chance and shown up. She tells him that, although she likes him, she needs a little notice. Besides, she has a man of her own—a black fellow Paulie has never seen because he's afraid to come to an Italian part of town. Even so, Orin promises Paulie that she will go out with him sometime. These comic and dramatic elements would have made for memorable moments, but at 132 minutes, *Jungle Fever* was already rather long and really shouldn't be any longer.

The most notorious deletion was also the most revealing. On the first page of his shooting script was a spoken introduction in which, in Spike's familiar, didactic direct-address mode, he would set us straight on what his movie was really about. Shot, then wisely left on the cutting-room floor, this opener indicates a lack of faith in the ability of his audience to make up their own minds. Didactic to the point of contempt, his proposed soliloquy went like this:

EXTERIOR:
BROOKLYN BRIDGE—SUNRISE

It's a bright clear fall morning and the director of this film, SPIKE LEE, descends from the sky riding in a CAMERA CRANE. He looks right INTO THE CAMERA and addresses the audience. He talks to us not as a character in this film but as the director:

SPIKE

All I have is [sic] questions. Very few of us have any real answers. Most have FALSE BOGUS ANSWERS, to FALSE SOLUTIONS [sic], Speakers of the UNTRUTH.
Questions.
Is a person a racist if he or she doesn't approve of interracial marriages or relationships?
Is White always gonna be ALRIGHT
And BLACK GET BACK?
Is the epitome of beauty in this world always gonna be the WHITE ANGLO-SAXON FEMALE?
Is the BLACK MALE the SUPERHUMAN SEXUAL STUD [sic] and that's all?
Are we ever gonna live together in peace?
Questions.

Spike rides up into the sky in the CAMERA CRANE as the morning sun glimmers on the Brooklyn Bridge.

Magically descending from the sky to deliver unto us his divine plan, Spike recalls Eli Cross (Peter O'Toole), the megalomaniacal moviemaker with the God complex in 1980's *The Stunt Man*. And in his need for a preface to clarify his intentions up front, he inadvertently triggers memories of phony TV-psychic Criswell's unintentionally hilarious foreword about UFO invasions in Edward D. Wood's 1959 camp classic *Plan 9 from Outer Space*. Especially Criswellian is the quasi-Biblical pompousness ("Speakers of the UNTRUTH"—who talks like that?) of Spike's wording.

No respectable director, no matter how explosive his subject matter, has ever felt the need to play Cinema Studies professor in his own movie as a preemptive strike against misinterpretation. Try to picture Stanley Kubrick personally warning patrons that, although *A Clockwork Orange* may *involve* violence, please be aware that it does not *endorse* violence. How about Akira Kurosawa adding a pre-title sequence to *The Seven Samurai* in which he delivers a lecture on the evils of feudalism? Even the pedantic Oliver Stone let *JFK* speak for itself. (And how did the Anglo-Saxons get in there when *Jungle Fever*'s female lead is of Italian descent?)

While he was up there on the crane, Spike also took the time to address those persistent charges of race-baiting that were lingering from the previous summer's *Mo' Better Blues*. Still in God-mode, Spike apologized to anyone he may have offended with his caricatures of the Jewish club owners Moe and Josh Flatbush. Staring sincerely into the lens, Spike began: "To those who've accused me of anti-Semitism," he said, holding up two fingers and making the peace-sign, "you can kiss my black ass, *two times!*" This is what's known as putting out fires with gasoline.

If Spike really felt the need to explain his movie before it had even begun, he'd have been better off with these lines from an introduction to a booklet of

Jungle Fever photos by his brother David Lee. He could have avoided the entire ugly camera-crane episode simply by setting the following in type:

> People put boundaries on each other.
> Some are real, some are imaginary.
> Sometimes when the boundaries of Race, Class
> and SEX are crossed,
> you are headed into that region [sic]
> called *JUNGLE FEVER*
>
> Spike Lee, 1991.

Other than its mistaking a fever for a region, this passage is not only much better written than the other intro, but doesn't leave the viewer feeling as though he or she is sitting at the back of third grade class, in the slow learners group.

By the time Spike Lee was making his fifth feature, he had been enough of an inspiration to young black people that some were embarking on their first film endeavors. One such striver was Matty Rich, who had written a script called *Straight Out of Brooklyn* and filmed it for peanuts around his Red Hook neighborhood. In the spring of 1991, Spike had heard the buzz in the filmmaking community about Rich's film. Spike decided to pay the young whippersnapper a visit. *Spy* magazine reported Spike's threat. "If your movie comes out at the same time as mine, I'll crush it!" As a result of this not-so-friendly visit, *Straight Out of Brooklyn* was rushed to screens by May 21 so as to comply with Spike's ultimatum. Matty Rich was nineteen at the time, child of the Brooklyn slums. As a thirty-four-year-old millionaire, Spike could not help looking

like a major-league bully. Not surprisingly, Rich
then went about being less than idolatrous to Spike in
interviews and, like his one-time idol, even opened
his own Brooklyn store.

In May of 1991, the struggles to make *Jungle
Fever* were over and Spike was ready to return to
the Cannes Film Festival—this time without Wim
Wenders. But two other people who had been targets
of Spike's wrath in the not-too-distant past were
present. Some saw this as poetic justice—a case of
Farmer Lee's chickens coming home to roost.

One was Alan Parker, director of *Mississippi
Burning*, a film Spike had accused of wantonly
rewriting civil rights history. The other was Whoopi
Goldberg, the popular star of *The Color Purple*,
whom Spike had loudly denounced for wearing
"motherfucking blue contact lenses." Would Parker
and Goldberg be biased against Spike? Would they
be able to put their past animosities behind them and
judge *Fever* strictly on its artistic merits?

In an *Empire* magazine interview, Parker reacted
strongly to the suggestion that he might have been
biased against Spike:

> That's just bollocks. There was certainly no
> controversy amongst the jury. In the end that
> jury is just ten people . . . from very different
> countries, backgrounds, cultures. And I don't
> remember Spike Lee getting more than one vote
> from anybody to be quite honest. Spike Lee is
> full of conspiracy theories because it's very
> easy, isn't it? He's not a very good filmmaker
> in my opinion. In many ways, from a technical

point of view, his work is not much different to films he was making at NYU with regards to his understanding of cinema. [And] what he's trying to say, I think it's very ugly—I think it's about hate, not love, it's about separatism not integration and I cannot go along with that."

Spike responded in the same issue. "You really *have* got to get away from this idea that these characters are representative of all black men and white women. Flipper and Angie do *not* represent every single couple in the world. Theirs is a relationship based on mutual curiosity."

Spike himself, however, claims no such curiosity: "I'm solely attracted to black women," he said. Is this genuinely his preference or is he, as Dap was in *School Daze*, "colorstruck" for darker sisters?

Did the director agree, the interviewer wanted to know, that *Fever* was a gentler film than *Do the Right Thing*? This seemed to set Spike off. "Gentler? *Gentler?* A father shoots his son in the stomach. A father beats the hell out of his daughter. This isn't a Walt Disney film, you know. And anyway, you don't judge a film by how *angry* it is or isn't."

Continuing the questioning about "this preoccupation with color," as a character in the film puts it, Spike was asked how *Jungle Fever* differs from *Do the Right Thing*—a leading question with racial implications if there ever were one. "I'm a better filmmaker than I was when I made *Do the Right Thing*," he snapped. *"That's* the difference between the two films."

Although the Cannes press conference was mainly stormy, there was also comic relief from an oafish journalist, who was either drunk or else suffering some sort of mental collapse in front of everyone. In the middle of a serious discussion of *Fever*'s grave concerns, that reporter suddenly and unexpectedly— apropos of nothing—struck Spike with the following statement: "White women have much bigger tits." Like most people in the room, Spike thought he must have misheard the question. Just in case they didn't catch it the first time, the journalist repeated his query. Undeterred, the questioner pressed on: "White women, Spike, have much bigger tits." Spike, his actors, and the hundred-odd members of the international press sat in stunned silence trying to figure out what point (if any) this reporter was trying to make. Panelists and journalists alike could not believe what they were hearing—or pretended not to. Luckily, someone across the room recognized the situation and changed the subject with a question about drugs.

Just how fair or unfair the balloting at Cannes was that spring is a matter of interpretation. "I learned my lesson in '89," Spike whined. "So I ain't expecting anything." As it happened, Spike *did* lose the Palme d'Or (again), this time to Joel and Ethan Coen's *Barton Fink*. Still, it was a good year for black film at Cannes: not just *Fever*, but *A Rage in Harlem* and *Boyz N the Hood* were also well received.

Jungle Fever did not, however, go home completely empty-handed. Cannes usually gives acting awards only for leading players, but the jury was so overwhelmed by Samuel L. Jackson's turn as the crackhead brother that they created a new supporting actor category just to honor him. In other words, so impressed were they by this little-known performer that they created a special one-time award just for Jackson.

Stateside, however, the Academy didn't even see fit to honor him with a nomination in an existing category. There are often differences in movie taste between the United States and Europe. But considering that American critics went out of their way to praise Jackson's acting, the Oscar snub was not due to translation problems. More Thinly Veiled Racism?Maybe—or just plain old Academy stupidity. (Something else to remember is that the Academy, based in L.A., has always favored its own, smug local heroes over their grittier, scrappier, East Coast competitors; New York movies always have a hard time at the Oscars solely because of the rivalry between the coasts.)

By this point in his career, Spike was getting to know his way around Hollywood's corridors of power. Although he was adept at working the system to his advantage, there were still aspects of it that rubbed him the wrong way. "It's funny," Spike observed in his book *Five for Five*, "the more films I do, the less it's about the film and the more it is about the deal." It may seem so to him, but to his credit, his films are less about "the deal" and more about what they're *supposed* to be about than nearly any other American director's. His movies may not always say what we want to hear, or say it the way we'd like to hear it, but each one is an original piece of work from an original mind. They are gutsy, scrappy pictures that are the antithesis of "the deal," and everyone who goes to the show for something other than popcorn is in his debt for this.

His progress in the industry has been more than merely a financial one. "I'm learning so much more with each film," he enthuses. "It's been said that directing films is like being a psychologist. It's so true."

Despite being described by a friend as "an art snob," Spike's tastes are generally unpretentious and down to earth. He doesn't care much for the theater and even less for performance art, dismissing most Off Broadway experimentation as "walk-on-the-stage-and-act-like-a-tree shit" and, more damning still, "what white people call art." He has struck that rare balance between the commercial and the creative that many filmmakers seek but few find.

For the first time, Spike did not publish a companion volume to accompany his film's release. Instead, he commissioned his brother David Lee to put together a book of still photos from all the joints. Entitled *Five for Five*, the picture book also contains essays from five prominent African-American writers, one for each from *She's Gotta Have It* through *Jungle Fever*.

Someone who wanted to be among that favored five was Amiri Baraka, the sixties leftover formerly known as LeRoi Jones—father of Lisa Jones, Spike's former collaborator. Baraka, an old-time Marxist and professional arguer, submitted an essay in which he trashed Spike Lee and his movies, mercilessly attacking them for not living up to a picture of black perfection—as exemplified, presumably, by Baraka himself.

Although Spike included essays that questioned some of his artistic choices over the years, clearly he wasn't about to put in his own book a contribution that did nothing but lash out at him. Whatever made Baraka think someone would *pay* for the privilege of being lambasted in print? It was an insulting thing even to attempt, but Spike simply passed on Baraka's manuscript and let the incident go. Spike didn't want to start something. The ex-Mr. Jones, however, plainly did.

Chapter 13

1991:
Outdo the Right Thing

Jungle Fever was released on June 7, 1991 (two weeks after *Straight Out of Brooklyn*), to generally favorable reaction and a strong opening. Eventually, it would gross $32 million—more than any Spike Lee movie to date, making good on the director's "five for five" claim of five hits with five films. But no Spike Lee film can simply creep into town, make a pile of money, and creep out again. By this time, we expect no less than a media storm every time Spike is at bat.

If *Jungle Fever* didn't shake things up quite as much Spike had anticipated, it still created a fair amount of turbulence. It's possible that by 1991 interracial romance was no longer the emotional firecracker that Spike had predicted. *Jungle Fever* generated many an editorial and commentary

("Lee is accused of consistently presenting Blacks in a way so negative as to conjure up images of Blacks from long-ago Hollywood films," reported African-American columnist Earl Caldwell in the August 12, 1991 New York *Daily News*), though fewer than *Do the Right Thing* had done two years earlier.

Flipper (Wesley Snipes) and Drew Purify (Lonette McKee) are thirtyish Buppies, raising their ten-year-old daughter Ming: they appear to be the ideal African-American family. In a brownstone on Strivers' Row, traditionally the most desirable part of Harlem, they still come face-to-face with many of the horrors of modern urban America. But, generally speaking, they have things pretty good.

His beloved (black) secretary having just left the company, Flipper complains that he had requested another African-American for the job. He is not pleased to meet Angie, with her lack of education and her Brooklyn accent. To his complaints, Flipper's boss snaps back, "Sounds suspiciously like reverse racism to me." Many would agree that it is— except, of course, that Spike believes black people are genetically incapable of racism: "I don't think Blacks can be racist," he said at Cannes in 1989. "Racism is where you put laws into effect, structures that effect you socially." ("It was a definite case of racism" is a kind of mantra running through Spike Lee's interviews and books.)

Angela Tucci of Bensonhurst was sent to temp at Mast and Covington, the midtown architectural firm where Flipper works. At the end of the first day, Flipper and Angie order Chinese food and get to know each other better. Sitting around the office, they inevitably talk about color. Before they've even cracked open their fortune cookies, the pair has been struck down with jungle fever: they're checking for "protection" and climbing onto the drafting table.

Flip and Angie each "confess" this interlude to their best friends—none of whom can keep a secret. Loved ones find out about this illicit liaison, and in two parts of town, all hell breaks loose. Angie is shunned by her family. Flipper is bounced from his house in the most embarrassing and public way imaginable. Flipper's parents, the Good Reverend Doctor and Mrs. Purify, invite the odd couple to their sturdy Harlem home for what turns out to be a mind game of the Reverend's called Guess Who's Not Coming to Dinner. The Rev. Purify has no sooner sat down at the table when he launches into a history lesson about how light-skinned blacks got that way not through evolution, but through the rape of slaves by their owners. Although the Reverend speaks slowly and calmly, there's no mistaking the anger in his hectoring lecture. Eventually, he rises and says he doesn't eat with "whoremongers." Angie is understandably taken aback by all this and Flip, profoundly embarrassed, escorts her out.

There are many things about Angie that could intrigue Flip. For one, she cooks for her family, perhaps inspiring in him a longing for a woman more traditional than the career woman he had married. For Flipper, Angie is different from his wife in ways that go well beyond skin color.

By contrast, Flipper's wife warns him against waking "the baby" when he's making love to her. She goes berserk at his first infidelity—not just throwing him out of the house, but also making sure the whole street knows about it and allowing his possessions to be damaged or stolen. After years of faithfulness, she's ready to end the marriage over a silly fling. When Flip takes flowers to her office and tries to apologize, she refuses to listen. Even after the white villainess is off the scene, she won't let her husband move back in! It may not have been Spike's intention to have the wife come across as so difficult to like—his script indicates only that they're supposed to be happily married. What we see of her, however, suggests that Flip has other reasons to be tempted by the fruit of another: Drew is a shrew.

Things aren't much better in Bensonhurst: everybody is unhappy, and for many of the same reasons. Families are turned against themselves, primarily because of the unreasonable demands of the older generation. In this, Spike shows there is no difference between the races: the grumpy and/or stifling old person is just a fact of human nature. Both Angie's and Paulie's fathers moan about how things were better when their wives were alive and how their children are disappointments to them.

Paulie is one of the most fascinating characters Spike Lee has ever created. Obviously intelligent and sensitive, he is wasting away his young life tending the cash register in his father's candy shop and taking abuse from the bigoted neighborhood pinheads. As none of them seems to work, this abuse goes on all day long. One of the shop's regulars goes berserk at the suggestion that his olive complexion and kinky hair might suggest a black ancestor somewhere in his family tree.

In addition to the excellent work of Annabella Sciorra and Wesley Snipes, Spike's supporting cast was even stronger than usual. He pulled an affecting performance from John Turturro as the mild-mannered Paulie and a hammy one from Anthony Quinn, while Ossie Davis and Ruby Dee as the Good Reverend Doctor and his long-suffering wife Lucinda are both superb. Tyra Ferrell as Orin, seemingly the only person in Bensonhurst besides Paulie whose IQ score runs to three digits, is also terrific.

And then there's the sad case called Gator. *Fever*'s finest moments arise from the tremendous performance given by Samuel L. Jackson as Flipper's older but not wiser crackhead brother. Simultaneously hilarious and frightening, Jackson's ability to capture the chronic user's vague, unfocused stare is itself worth the price of admission. The climactic moments between Gator and his father are, along with the Taj Mahal sequence and *Do the Right Thing*'s riot, the most shattering few feet of film Spike Lee has ever run through a camera. (Spike has said that the event was inspired by the 1984 death of Marvin Gaye, who had also had a history of drug use and who also was shot by his preacher father.)

Spike makes all of Gator's scenes reverberate with an authenticity that is truly remarkable for someone with no firsthand experience of drugs. Knowing what we do now, however, about Spike's father Bill Lee and his heroin habit, we can speculate that some of what Spike might have gone through with his own father may have inspired these scenes in *Jungle Fever*. Spike has always been vehemently anti-drug—right from the credits for *She's Gotta Have It*—and has identified the crack problem as being "tied directly to the destruction of the black family." Although *Jungle Fever*, the only Lee film to address the drug question, didn't preach against them, it would take a very unusual person to sit through the gruelling "Taj Mahal" sequence and still want, in Spike words, to "suck on that glass dick."

"That particular scene [of the colossal crackhouse called the Taj Mahal] is artistic license," Spike readily admitted to *Empire*. "There aren't any places that I know that are on quite as big a scale as the Taj Ma-, hal, but I portrayed it that size to ram home just how bad the situation is. The fact that is the one place where I took artistic license does not negate how severe the situation is right now. Crack is wiping out generations and generations of people.

"I just don't know how to address the whole drugs issue more head-on than I do with *Jungle Fever*." So powerfully does *Jungle Fever* take on the issue that the drug subplot even threatens to upstage the main story of Flipper and Angie.

Jungle Fever offers many delights, not the least of which are an original score by Terence Blanchard and a fine batch of Stevie Wonder songs: mostly new material as well as Wonder's 1973 classic "Livin' for the City" for the harrowing Taj Mahal scene.

Spike's characters have always had colorful names. The ones he's given just to Joie Lee's characters—Clorinda, Lizzie Life, Jade and Indigo—sound like something that might have been inflicted on the Exotic Colored Chanteuse in a bozo musical from the 1940s. His men don't get off any lighter, with a Runyonesque catalogue including Mars, Half-Pint, Big Brother Almigh-tee, Doo-Doo

Breath, Double Rubber, Dap, Mister Señor Love Daddy, Da Mayor, Mookie, Punchy, ML (which, we're told, stands for nothing more than just ML), Coconut Sid, Sweet Dick Willie, Giant, Left-Hand Lacey, Bleek, Shadow, Butterbean, Bottom Hammer, Big Stop, Rhythm, Eggy, and Born Knowledge. They may be improbable, but they're certainly memorable.

With *Jungle Fever*, however, Spike outdid himself when he named Wesley Snipes's character "Flipper Purify." Angie takes note of his peculiar moniker (who wouldn't?), but Flip can't account for it other than to blame it on his father's eccentricity. (Considering this man christened his other son Gator and himself insists on being addressed as "The Good Reverend Doctor," we have no reason to doubt this explanation.) The "Flipper" part has no apparent symbolic value; the "Purify" part broadcasts its symbolism with a megaphone.

Spike doesn't fare quite so well with portraying black professional life. His character Cyrus is a high school teacher, though we never see him at work. Cyrus's pretty mulatto wife has even fewer scenes; we never get an idea of what she's all about.

Once again, Spike leans to loading the deck: he still tends to see issues in (it has to be said) black and white. The problem is not so much that Flipper and Angie must represent all mixed-race couples, but that there is considerably more complexity to the issue than *Fever* ever gets around to investigating. The status symbol that a white woman can represent for a black man is fairly clear, however illusory and destructive that symbolism may ultimately be. But the status the black man confers on the white woman is not at all clear. From her peers, she may elicit outward disgust and secret admiration—or outward admiration and secret disgust.

White men with black women is even more complex, but don't expect to learn anything about it from *Jungle Fever*. Spike starts then apparently loses interest in a subplot about Paulie's attraction to a pretty black customer, leaving the outcome up in the air. If Flip and Angie are exclusively about sex, *this* couple is strangely sexless.

Black men's self-loathing over having been roped in by the European standard of beauty is unquestionably a minefield of a subject—and perfect for a cinematic kamikaze pilot like Spike. But it's hard to leave *Jungle Fever* without feeling unsatisfied both artistically and politically.

There is another way to look at *Jungle Fever*. Maybe what unifies these seemingly disparate plot lines is the notion of the dysfunctional family. Of the film's three families, two are headed by widowers and the third by a religious maniac. Racial matters aside, loony domestic behavior is scarcely something confined to Blacks, just as Caucasians don't own the generation gap. *Fever*'s scenes of intergenerational conflict are well scripted and powerfully performed, with the Rev. and Flipper, in particular, emerging as men of vastly different eras and social experience—and consequently different ways of interpreting the world around them. Maybe *Jungle Fever* is less about interracial relationships than about black self-hatred: the use of crack, self-victimization and other self-destructive behavior all fall under the category of black people doing stupid things to themselves.

With *Jungle Fever*, Spike's attitude toward and his use of female characters became a more critical issue. How do women feel about Spike's movies? Well, with the exception of *She's Gotta Have It*, they generally don't feel too good. The perception remains, rightly or wrongly, that his female characters are sketchily developed when they're not outright stereotypes. Not even the frank, lusty, all-girl kaffee klatsch in *Jungle Fever* seemed to help the situation. Rosie Perez's Tina in *Do the Right Thing* is certainly a strong, memorable female character, but if she does anything in her life besides scream at Mookie, we don't get to know about it.

The "boundaries" Spike talked about crossing with this film are only the boundaries that artists cross all the time. Crossing borders is not in itself either brave or artistic: it's what you bring back from the other side that counts.

So what did Spike Lee bring back from the other side? With what dazzling insights and vanguard visions did he return? That penis size does not matter, except of course to white women who have historically been deprived of black men? That when Italian-Americans forbid their children to date African-Americans, they're bigoted brutes; but when African-Americans forbid *their* children to date Italian-Americans, they're preserving their heritage and the purity of their blood? That genuine love and affection is not possible between the races, because Whites always operate from selfish motives? That the races should keep to themselves,'cause there'll only be trouble if they don't? Questions.

Someone who wants to get rid of stereotypes must be prepared to get rid of *all* of them, not just the unflattering ones; it's not a matter of picking and choosing. True liberation can come only from everyone's insistence on equality and fairness. The idea is to free ourselves from the racial superstition, misinformation and myth-making of the past—not to perpetuate them.

But at the height of number five's popularity, Spike was already too busy working on number six: *Malcolm X* would take all the concentration he could muster.

Chapter 14

1991: Let X = X

Back in February of 1990, Spike spoke to a packed house at the Newark Public Library as part of their regular question-and-answer sessions. With him was Ernest Dickerson, a Newark native welcomed home by a standing-room-only crowd. It was also the occasion of the twenty-fifth anniversary of Malcolm X's death. Inevitably, the two were asked about the rumored Malcolm movie—which at that time seemed safely in the hands of Norman Jewison, the Canadian-born director of *In the Heat of the Night*, *Moonstruck*, and *Other People's Money*. "I'm not involved in the project at this time," replied Spike. "Supposedly, something might happen where I will be involved."

Something might happen? It was no secret that Spike was out there trying to *make* something happen. He wanted control of the movie and was campaigning hard behind Jewison's back to take over the project. Spike Lee wanted *Malcolm X* the way Oliver Stone had wanted *JFK*. And to get it, he put Malcolm's dictum "By any means necessary" into action.

"If there's a film I'm looking forward to even less than *JFK*, it's *Malcolm X*," lamented a New York journalist at a press luncheon as 1991 lurched wearily into 1992. "Just imagine—Spike Lee bashing Whitey over the head for *three hours!*" Although this scribe was guilty of judging a film in advance, he was right about one thing: *Malcolm X* is Spike Lee's *JFK*. And the real-life Malcolm is to Spike what John Fitzgerald Kennedy is to Oliver Stone: someone the director has taken as his inspiration, admired and idolized—maybe even a little too much. Malcolm X and John F. Kennedy are to their film biographers no less than Christ-figures, and their film biographies are nothing less than high-profile, career-threatening personal crusades.

When Stone's *JFK* was released just before Christmas of 1991, it immediately begat bitter bickering unseen in the movie world since . . . well, since *Do the Right Thing*. Like Spike, Stone was riding a successful wave of such "big" movies on touchy topics (*Platoon*, *Wall Street*, *Talk Radio*, *Born on the Fourth of July*) and now wanted to crown his career with the biggest and most explosive of all such films. However many feathers Spike might rustle with *Malcolm X*, he can rest safe in the knowledge that Oliver Stone has rustled even more. When it comes to upsetting people, implicating Lyndon Johnson, the mafia and the CIA in a conspiracy to kill Kennedy so as to prolong the Vietnam War and enrich the military-industrial complex, this is a tough one to top.

Apart from Spike and Stone, there are significant parallels between Malcolm X and John Kennedy themselves: Malcolm was at the peak of his influence and popularity during Kennedy's administration and was assassinated only fifteen months after the late president. Furthermore, a turning point in Malcolm's life came when he described the killing of the President as a case of "the chickens coming home to roost" (i.e., the violence and hatred of America had finally taken the life of its own leader). This remark, after Malcolm's spiritual mentor the Honorable Elijah Muhammad had forbidden American Muslims from commenting on the assassination, was given as the reason Minister Malcolm and the Honorable Elijah Muhammad parted company—a claim Malcolm strenuously disputed.

"We're delighted for Oliver Stone [that *JFK* is a hit]," said Spike in the *New York Post*, "because now Warners can't give us a hard time about the length [of *Malcolm X*]." Like *JFK*, Spike's Malcolm bio-pic is expected to break the dreaded three-hour mark—a full hour longer than studios usually like their movies to be. (Running times of more than two hours make it difficult for cinemas to program two shows per evening, thereby endangering the exhibitors' profitability.) And, like Stone, all Spike's supporters will be prepared to hail it as a masterpiece, while all his enemies will be poised to pounce. Everybody, friend and foe, wants to know: Can Spike capture the personality of this multi-faceted, brilliant and often exasperating man named Malcolm? Is he gonna be able to pull off The Big One?

"*The Autobiography of Malcolm X* is an American literary classic that has enriched the lives of many readers," writes Clayborne Carson in his 1991 book, *Malcolm X: The FBI File*. "But it is less successful as social and political history. . . . All serious study of Malcolm X must begin with his autobiography; unfortunately, many works on him do not extend beyond the biographical and historical information provided by Malcolm himself."

So what about Spike Lee's work on Malcolm? He had for years been itching to document the life of the fiery activist—as had a number of other prominent individuals, both black and white. The question was, who would win the privilege? Warner Brothers had long owned the rights to *The Autobiography of Malcolm X*. Producer Marvin Worth bought the rights to the sensational volume (as told to the late *Roots* author Alex Haley) from Malcolm's widow, Dr. Betty Shabazz, back in 1967. Who would direct the film was uncertain, but this much was clear: the studio to produce it would definitely be Warners. The sum total of Spike's previous contact with Warners was to infuriate them by giving away the ending of *Bonfire of the Vanities*. But in Hollywood, anything can be forgiven as long as the money keeps flowing—and Spike Lee has been doing just that since Day One.

There was still the matter of the script. In the ensuing two decades, many had tried—and failed—to "lick" the *Autobiography*'s sprawling 400 pages and fashion it into a screenplay that was both truthful as history and satisfactory as drama. Spike felt he could succeed where others before him had failed—among them black playwright Charles

Fuller (*A Soldier's Story*), black novelists David
Bradley (*The Chaneysville Incident*) and Calder
Willingham (*Eternal Fire*), and even David Mamet,
the white playwright (*Sexual Perversity in Chicago*)
and filmmaker (*Homicide, House of Games*). Spike
had read the last of these back in 1987, reporting, "I
like David Mamet's script, but I would have to write
my own." He dismissed another screen adaptation as
reading "like a TV movie."

The general feeling was that the attempt which
came closest to the target was the one by esteemed
black writer James Baldwin (*Notes of a Native Son,
Go Tell It on The Mountain, Another Country*)—
who had the advantage of having known Malcolm
personally—which had been completed by Arnold
Perl. For one reason or another, each attempt to film
the *Autobiography* had reached an impasse: there
was no doubt that Malcolm's engrossing, inspira-
tional and frequently bizarre life belonged on the
silver screen, but getting it there was a daunting task
for a number of reasons.

According to a *Daily News* interview, Spike chose
to take the Baldwin-Perl version and give it his
own treatment. "I thought it was a great script
except for the last third—because a lot of history about Malcolm's assassination has come out
since it was completed." And, "Of all the scripts
I read, the Baldwin was the best. But the final
act was kind of weak. At the time he wrote it,
the Honorable Elijah Muhammad was still alive,
and a lot of stuff about the assassination and their
split was not public knowledge. Baldwin was very
leery about it. That was 1969; now it's 1991. The
research is out."

James Baldwin himself had once said that "a Malcolm movie being made by white Hollywood is unthinkable." In the 1960s, he was right. In the 1990s, it's not only thinkable, but probable. As an indication of how pervasive Malcolm X has become, consider a 1991 episode of the Fox TV sitcom *True Colors* in which fourteen-year-old Lester reads the *Autobiography*, discovers his True Black Self, and changes his name to Abdul X (which is TV non-sense, as he would have to undergo a conversion to Islam first). Lester then becomes a self-righteous pain in the ass to both sides of his interracial family. So, some time between the civil rights 1960s and the new jack 1990s, Malcolm's recognition factor increased from cult figure to household word, prime time plot thickener. For better or for worse, Malcolm's importance has eclipsed Martin Luther King's in the hearts and minds of today's African-American youth. Considering the 'X' baseball cap that presently adorns millions of heads, there is clearly much grass roots demand for more and more Malcolm.

Martin got his own national holiday, but Malcolm's getting his own movie. Yet, who should be the one to direct it? Spike believed that he passed the most important qualifier.

In the July 1991 *Playboy* he explained this sentiment. "I am of the opinion that only a Black man should write and direct *The Autobiography of Malcolm X*. Bottom line." In an unfortunate replay of the old can-white-men-play-the-blues dilemma, Norman Jewison tried to defend his right to make a Malcolm bio-pic. In early 1991, Jewison was just about ready to go, using the script by Charles

Fuller (whose *A Soldier's Story* Jewison had vividly brought to the screen in 1984).

Jewison, known as one of few white directors to treat black issues with intelligence and sensitivity, took exception to the race-based nature of Spike's arguments. "I can't agree with Spike Lee," he said on Canadian television in 1991. "That's an apartheid statement. For any artist to say that another artist can't cope with a story because of skin color is ridiculous. The reason I dropped out of making a Malcolm X story is that I couldn't lick the script. But there've been five other screenplay attempts that couldn't lick that story, either."

What finally swung Warner's decision over to Spike had less to do with morality than with economics: having a black director at the helm of a film about Malcolm X's life was not only more appropriate, it also made more box-office sense. Jewison is a director with a fair financial record, offsetting his occasional losers (*In Country, Best Friends*) with enough winners (*Moonstruck, In the Heat of the Night*) to keep him working steadily for more than three decades. But as popular and as influential as Malcolm has recently become, an epic biography of this size would need to be able to attract customers not just because of who it was about, but also because of who was behind it. Millions of moviegoers would want to see any Malcolm movie—but millions more would want to see Spike Lee's version.

As Spike is fond of pointing out, all of his films have made money. He has probably a larger loyal following—folks who can be relied on to turn out for *anything* he might come up with—than any other filmmaker alive. (Woody Allen, for instance, is also considered as having a faithful audience, yet several of his films have failed so badly that their ticket sales never even crept into the seven-figure range, let alone eight or nine. The 1987 drama *September*, for instance, netted its studio a pathetic $160,000 theatrically.)

In other words, a Malcolm X movie made by Norman Jewison would have going for it only its dynamic subject matter. A Malcolm X movie made by Spike Lee would have going for it not only that same dynamic subject but also a writer-director-actor with a huge and intense fan club. South Africa's Steven Biko was also a hero to millions when British director Richard Attenborough (*Gandhi*) made his Biko bio-pic, *Cry Freedom*, in 1987. Despite good reviews—and the presence of Denzel Washington—*Cry Freedom* was a financial disaster. No doubt the studio was afraid the same might happen to a Malcolm movie flown by a white pilot.

A sense of historical inevitability, of a *mission*, informs all of Spike's thinking about Malcolm X: "I think this is the right time for this film to be done," he has said. Furthermore, "I don't think it's any coincidence that several other filmmakers have tried to make *The Autobiography* before and, right now, it happens. I feel this film is supposed to be made right now."

And, presumably, it's supposed to be made by Spike Lee.

Throughout the summer of 1991, Spike was deep in prep for what would be by far the biggest shoot

of his life—and, for that matter, one of the bigger
undertakings of the movie year. Upon rising each
morning throughout that summer, Spike would write
for four hours and *then* go about the myriad of other tasks required to launch a movie of *Malcolm's*
magnitude. Despite his best efforts at damage
control, the logistical nightmare of managing the
hundreds of individuals and thousands of details in
Malcolm X would soon turn it into Spike's most
troubled and frustrating shoot ever.

Although *Malcolm X*'s $33.5 million isn't quite
the $88 million swagbag director James Cameron
somehow managed to empty for *Terminator 2*, it
nonetheless represents a taller stack of greenbacks
than most filmmakers ever get to see in one place.
Even if Spike were making something as safe and
as bland as, say, *Twins VII*, with that kind of money, all of Hollywood would still be watching him
closely just because of the huge sums involved.
That Spike was putting those funds to use in the
service of someone the U.S. government deemed a
dangerous radical and an enemy of the state meant
scrutiny not just from the movie industry, but from
the entire nation. Spike-watchers beefed up their
vigilance, training their binoculars on him even
more intently than usual. Anything even remote-
ly connected with Spike and his project suddenly
became newsworthy.

"Somebody could definitely be *killed* behind this
movie. Hopefully, it won't be me." So said Spike to
a *Vanity Fair* reporter early in 1991. Someone did. A
young black woman named Shona Bailey, who was
working as an extra in *Malcolm's* crowd scenes, did
in fact die before finishing her scenes—though, con-

trary to how it was portrayed in the media, her death had nothing to do with *Malcolm X*. The truth is simply that one night after leaving the set, somewhere between her cab and the door of her Harlem apartment, Bailey was killed by an unknown assailant. As tragic as this young woman's untimely passing was, it was only one of five such homicides that New York City racks up every day of the year. Like Bill Lee's drug bust, the Bailey story was one with little inherent news value—unless linked to someone of Spike Lee's star power. Spike's fame has reached a level at which the press follows his every move—and those of everyone connected with him. Not all of these people, needless to say, have Spike Lee's best interests at heart.

This minute inspection applies not only to events involving Spike, but also to the man himself. An attack published in *GQ* in 1990 had ridiculed Spike for acting like "Malcolm X with a distribution deal." Although a cruel jab, Spike had been inviting it by his concerted effort to fuse his own image with that of the martyred Malcolm. Spike had also borrowed the Malcolmism "By Any Means Necessary" as his slogan for his filmworks since it had been incorporated. More recently, he's been bordering his mouth with a neatly trimmed goatee and his eyes with shiny, narrow-framed 1950s corrective lenses.

And, not content merely to sport the same embroidered 'X' cap as millions of other young Blacks, Spike had to go that extra step by accessorizing his with a small rectangular button emblazoned with a photo catching Malcolm in mid-speech fury. Through everything from Spike's black-solidarity pronouncements to his personal appearance, there does seem to have been a concentrated effort to narrow the gap between the two men. But measured against Malcolm, whether by yardstick or by IQ test, Spike can't fail to come up short. The self-taught Malcolm, whose schooling ended at the eighth grade, possessed a command of the language and a more eloquent and memorable way of expressing his dissatisfactions than does Spike, who had the benefit of attending not one but two respected universities. Compared to the penetrating clarity of Malcolm's analyses and his devastating critiques of historical injustices, Spike's pronouncements are strictly from bumper-stickers: their shock value is as essential as their content.

To solidify even further this Spike-Malcolm connection in the eyes of the public, Spike contributed an Introduction to *Malcolm X: The FBI File*, a collection of previously suppressed government data from the early fifties through the mid-sixties. Spike's remarks were brief and predictably inflammatory, complete with sweeping generalizations and unsubstantiated accusations. He described America in classic Professor Griff language as "a wicked country," then accused the FBI, CIA and police of having been "in cahoots" with the Nation of Islam to assassinate Malcolm X—among many, many others:

Who else? King? Both Kennedys? Evers? Hampton? The list goes on and on. J. Edgar Hoover was a known racist and he did all he could and more to stop any movement by or on behalf of Blacks, all under the guise of protecting democracy.

Spike is right about Hoover's racism, but reckless remarks like the one alleging an FBI-CIA-NOI conspiracy consistently get Spike into difficulties. These claims may or may not prove to have foundation in truth, but until Spike knows for certain, he would be wise to reserve judgment.

"The white man's got a God complex," chanted seventies proto-rap group The Last Poets. True enough, but perhaps Spike Lee's got a Malcolm complex. He clearly wants not only to be known as a great filmmaker, but also as a Great Man. "I never aspired to be the black spokesman," he claimed in vain in *Playboy*. This is, after all, a man who named one of his books *Uplift the Race*.

But whatever questions about Spike might linger, his subject matter is solid: Malcolm X was a populist prophet, and the time is past due for a serious screen examination.

He was born Malcolm Little in Omaha, Nebraska, on May 19, 1925. Forty years later, he died as El-Hajj Malik El Shabazz on February 21, 1965. He was, however, mostly known by neither of those names, but by the enigmatic moniker Malcolm X. Converted to Islam while in prison for burglary, he was first a disciple, then an enemy, of Nation of Islam founder the Honorable Elijah Muhammad and first an enemy, and later a reluctant supporter, of the other key figure in twentieth-century black America, Martin Luther King, Jr. Often dubbed "the angriest black man in America" and "hero of the black man, bane of the white man," Malcolm X was the subject of extensive FBI documentation. This devoted husband and father remains a potent symbol of black empowerment to millions of people.

In just under forty years, Malcolm X did enough living for several lifetimes, and seemingly as several different individuals. His preacher father, a follower of Jamaican-born Marcus Garvey, was murdered by Klansmen when Malcolm was only six years old. The family almost starved as Mrs. Little's sanity suffered under the strain; Malcolm and the other children were placed in foster care. In his teens, Malcolm drifted around the country—and into crime—before being arrested at 21. While imprisoned for a series of burglaries, Malcolm underwent a religious conversion, mostly at the prodding of his family, who had become involved with an American Islamic sect headed by Elijah Muhammad.

This eventually led to the changing of his "slave-master name," first to Malcolm X (during his Nation of Islam period) and later to Malik El Shabazz. According to *The Autobiography of Malcolm X*, Malcolm first supported then dramatically parted ways with Elijah Muhammad's Nation of Islam (NOI). The Nation of Islam was the preferred name for the group; Malcolm always disliked the term "Black Muslims" coined for them by the media. The American members prefer simply "Muslim"—even if the Muslims of the East consider their interpretation of the Koran to be idiosyncratic and inaccurate.

Malcolm was slain in February 1965 as he began a speech to his newly-formed Organization of Afro-American Unity (OAAU) at Harlem's Audubon Ballroom. Three black men firing handguns simultaneously at close range were arrested, though theories vary about their motives.

In his book *The Cool, Crazy, Committed World Of The Sixties*, long running Canadian television interviewer Pierre Berton wrote, "Malcolm X was a black racist. And his background suggests that he had good reason to be." Berton, who hosted Malcolm's final TV appearance in Toronto only one month before the assassination, went on to quote something strangely prescient: "I remember Dick Gregory telling me that [Malcolm X] was the most significant of all Negro leaders and would soon replace Dr. Martin Luther King as the real symbol of Negro resistance to white supremacy." Written in 1965, with Malcolm dead and Dr. King at his peak, this sentiment struck Berton as unlikely. Yet time seems to have vindicated Dick Gregory's prediction.

For many reasons, the pressure on Spike Lee to do justice to Malcolm's incredible life story is enormous. More eyes will be on Spike in this endeavor than for all his previous films combined.

At least in the casting department, things seem to be going Spike's way. Oscar-winning Denzel Washington, rising Hollywood heart-throb and star of Spike's own *Mo' Better Blues*, was chosen for the title role, in what will probably prove the role of a lifetime. In *The Autobiography*, Malcolm makes many mentions of his white grandfather, of his "high-yeller" mother, and of his own reddish complexion and hair. Washington, of course, has dark brown skin and ebony hair, although he does share Malcolm's tall, wiry physique and regal comportment. For the production, Washington had his hair dyed Malcolm's gingery.

For himself, Spike reserved the small but juicy role

of Shorty Henderson, a jazz-and-dope buddy from Malcolm's wild years in Boston in the 1940s. Shorty and Malcolm were sent to prison for burglary simultaneously—and for much longer sentences than were the thrill-seeking white girls who were their accomplices. Shorty is but a minor character in the book; perhaps not surprisingly, he has expanded to a larger one for the film.

Other performers include Lonette McKee (*Jungle Fever*) as Malcolm's widowed mother, Angela Bassett as Betty Shabazz, veteran character actor Peter Boyle (*Joe*) and even the Rev. Al Sharpton, the New York-based preacher-activist, as Malcolm's father. Marvin Worth, who got the ball rolling for a Malcolm movie back in the 1960s, shares producing chores with Monty Ross. The screenplay was finally credited to three names: James Baldwin, Arnold Perl and Spike Lee.

Having at last whipped the script into shape, Spike could then get on with preproduction. But at the beginning of August 1991, a meeting at Spike's house was interrupted by a knock at the door. Standing with a grimace on his face and "An Open Letter to Spike Lee" in his hand, was the black communist agitator Amiri Baraka. Baraka (formerly the poet-playwright LeRoi Jones) had clashed with Spike before over both ideological and personal matters and finally saw his chance to grab some press. He claimed to represent an organization called the United Front to Preserve the Legacy of Malcolm X and the Cultural Revolution. The Front, a hastily thrown-together congregation of aging sixties radicals, had this to say:

This letter is meant to begin to focus the whole of the black nation on Spike Lee's film about Malcolm X. This is entirely serious. We will not have our "shining black prince" distorted out of petty bourgeois ignorance, arrogance or lack of courage. This life of Malcolm X is not just a "commercial property," it is an expression of a people's life, will and history. And if Malcolm X's life is distorted or belittled or caricatured in any way, we will lead a struggle, from theater to theater across the country, if we have to, to see that the masses of black people are informed about what these distortions are, and what must be done to oppose and end them. . . . Our distress about Spike's making a film on Malcolm is based on our analysis of the films he has already made— their caricature of black people's lives, their dismissal of our struggle and the implication of their description of the black nation as a few besieged Buppies surrounded by an irresponsible repressive lumpen.

Despite the fall of Communism, Baraka still proudly identifies himself as a Marxist, as evidenced by his archaic worker's-struggle language ("petty bourgeois," "the masses," "lumpen") that not even the Kremlin uses anymore.

This black Stalin is apparently a frustrated film critic, also, and so took the opportunity to attack *Do the Right Thing* for having "reduced the Black Liberation Movement to a comic burlesque demanding black flicks [sic] in a pizza parlor led by Bugging

[sic] Out. It told us as well that our children were killed in our caricatured Hill St. Blues community only for playing their radio too loud." Baraka also gave the thumbs-down to *She's Gotta Have It*, with the absurd complaint that "it transformed the black woman's movement for equality into nymphomania." *School Daze* "trashed black colleges as colored Animal Houses existing strictly for copulation and rock where students were either wanna be whites or else they were just dark jealous jigaboos and hypocritical militants who wanna be wannabes." (It should be recalled that Baraka had never liked Spike since he became a close friend and collaborator of his daughter, Lisa Jones.)

But Spike is too good at arguing to let a challenge like that go by without a stinging rebuttal. In an *Emerge* magazine interview he struck back. "While I respect the concerns of the writers of the letter, this film will not be made by committee." He then proceeded to fire a series of a well-aimed blasts at his opponent's pretensions, striking Baraka right in the credentials: "When Malcolm was assassinated in 1965, I was eight years old. Amiri Baraka was calling himself LeRoi Jones and was running around Greenwich Village with Allen Ginsberg being a beatnik. He didn't even move uptown to Harlem until after Malcolm was assassinated! I don't tell Baraka what to write in his books, and he can't tell me what to say in my films."

Spike defended himself against Amiri Baraka's charges that his "exploitation film" was trivializing Malcolm's life, in Baraka's words, "to make middle-class Negroes sleep easier." To which Spike spat back, "Even though Mr. Baraka has appointed himself the grand pooh-bah of all blacks, artists don't do that. There are 30 million blacks in this country. I think more are on my side than his." In short, Spike summed up, "Baraka is full of shit."

In a calmer mood, Spike allowed as how "we know we can't satisfy everybody's vision of Malcolm X. He has achieved mythic proportions . . . but we knew going into it we'd have that problem [of trying to be all things to all people]." Instead of knocking himself out trying to cover all the bases, Spike sensibly set himself the more realistic goals of "being as honest as possible" and "to make a great film."

The Spike Lee version of *Malcolm X* may or may not be a great film, but it will *not* be an exploitation film and it will *not* trash Malcolm's life. And, considering all this mayhem happened before Spike had the chance to shoot a single frame of film, nobody is going to sleep easier.

Chapter 15

1991–92: Project X

When Spike Lee hired the Fruit of Islam for security on *Do The Right Thing* in 1988, he may have had more in mind that just an Afrocentric alternative to the NYPD; he may already have been thinking ahead to *Malcolm X*. By winning the respect of American Muslims, the group might not be so quick to judge Spike when he came to chronicle their most famous member. Knowing how such a film might anger the NOI, Spike may have recognized the importance of maintaining cordial relations with them—especially since Minister Louis Farrakhan, in his humbler days as Brother Louis X in the early sixties, had called for the death of the "traitor" Malcolm X in the official Muslim newspaper *The Messenger*. "This," Spike said in the August 12, 1991 *Daily News*, "is one set the Fruit will definitely *not* be guarding."

At first, the Nation of Islam kept uncharacteristically quiet on the subject of a Malcolm movie. Minister Farrakhan did not return Spike's phone calls and made no public statements about the project. Finally, however, in the summer of 1991, as Spike was getting ready to start shooting, Spike was granted an audience with Louis Farrakhan himself. The reverend—who is to America's Black Muslims what the pope is to Roman Catholics—obviously has much to lose if perceived as having been against this increasingly popular and influential figure.

When a reporter confronted Farrakhan with his own words in *The Messenger*—which amounted to a death threat—in an August 1990 interview in the black news-and-politics magazine, *Emerge*, the minister broke down and cried. His inflammatory article of twenty-five years before, he pleaded, was just "the climate of the times." Looking back, he reflected, "I would do it differently if I had to do it over again."

Because these past hostilities between Malcolm and Farrakhan were well known, Spike was somewhat apprehensive going in to the interview. Yet he found Farrakhan gracious and helpful. Unlike the administration at his old alma mater Morehouse, Farrakhan "did not ask to see the script or anything. He just said, 'Listen to everybody's truth, Spike, pray, and then come up with your own truth.' " Spike took the advice and got back to work. He even vowed he'd turn to Farrakhan for help if things got too rough in his next battle—for Spike's 1991 fight-card was not yet completely filled in.

This time Spike was going to war with the Teamsters, the union of film craftspeople. According to Spike, the union—the most powerful in the entertainment industry—was still not cooperating with his request that more black technicians should be admitted to their ranks. Spike claimed that the last black Teamster to get his "book"—that is, become an official member, with full benefits—had been in 1962! Yet with 175 speaking parts and shooting to occur on two continents, this was much too big a movie for the Teamsters to resist. A whole lot of dues could be collected from this one, and the union was determined not to miss out on any of it.

Spike was clearly concerned about Teamster retaliation. At one point, he was threatening that, should the feud not be resolved peacefully, he and his people would be prepared to defend the *Malcolm X* set physically if the Teamsters tried to disrupt his shoot. He said he would seek solidarity and help not only from Farrakhan but also from Mayor Dinkins and Police Commissioner Lee Brown should the conflict come to blows. In the meantime Spike, with his patented brand of belligerence, taunted that the Teamsters could "Kiss my ass, *two* times!"

Eventually, a compromise was reached by which the Teamsters would work on *Malcolm X*—and some new union cards would be issued to African-Americans. So in came the Teamsters, a little more deeply complected than usual. The most integrated Teamsters crew in history was soon, like the mostly African-American cast, referring to the project simply as *X*.

But Spike's troubles were not over yet: like the Hydra, no sooner could he slice off one snarling head when two more would appear. The sheer size of it meant *Malcolm X* would be a daunting undertaking. It soon turned out to be the most unwieldy, problematic and crisis-ridden project Spike Lee has ever had to pilot. Although Spike has taken the odd misstep, he's never stumbled so badly that he couldn't get up again.

In the meantime, however, Spike found time for a little fun. In late September, Spike guested on *Saturday Night Live* in a skit about a fictitious cable show hosted by Black militant Nat X (Chris Rock). The cantankerous filmmaker, a walking billboard for Spike's Joint in full *Malcolm X* regalia, played his favorite role: himself. It was a fairly limp sketch, ill-suited to Spike's comic abilities. In one of the scene's brighter moments, Nat X scolded Spike for having used the white Annabella Sciorra in *Jungle Fever*. Why couldn't the role have gone to a black actress, Nat demanded, "considering how many sisters out there need the work." Nat also asked Spike what he was working on at the moment. Spike replied that he was about to start shooting the Malcolm X story with Denzel Washington. "And," he assured us, "we hope to win the Oscar with this one." In other words, Spike was making noise about winning an Oscar before he'd even made the movie! Now *here* was an opportunity for humor—though not one the dreary latter-day *SNL* would be quick enough to pick up on.

After Spike's night of self-publicity on TV, it was time to start the serious business of mounting an epic. From September through December, Spike and company shot the American segments in Harlem and midtown Manhattan (which also doubled as Boston), as Malcolm's saga twisted through his pimping, dealing, gambling—and eventually to his spiritual rebirth in the Muslim faith in a New England prison. The first month of the new year would take them to Africa for the rest.

Actors and extras report the on-set Spike was quieter than usual—sullenly silent, sometimes—and never ventured far from the camera. Some describe him as seeming harried and distracted, while others assess his on-set demeanor as simply efficient and businesslike. Some found him to be brusque and curt, even to the point of rudeness. It was apparent that Spike was in a hurry to do *Malcolm* and that the whole production was not sufficiently prepared.

Spike has never stuck so rigidly to the storyboard that he wouldn't consider suggestions from his cast, but adding entirely new scenes to *X* at the last moment was a sign of previously unseen desperation. Noticing that his script mentioned the FBI keeping surveillance on Malcolm but didn't actually show it, it struck Spike that the audience might think Malcolm was merely paranoid. He decided, therefore, he needed to come up with a scene in which two agents (one of whom is played by *Brother from Another Planet* writer-director John Sayles) monitor Malcolm's activities with a tape recorder from a hotel room. For this and other late additions, actors had to work without a script and simply ad lib their lines.

Despite the air of barely controlled panic, the general atmosphere on the set was still very professional, according to those who worked on it. The pressures of his ever-expanding budget, however, did make Spike less friendly and outgoing than he has been in the past. It's nothing new for Spike's crews to want a more attentive, warm, and giving leader, but during *X* he was even more remote than usual toward everyone but his cameraman and his star. There seems to be a consensus that he still doesn't have a lot of tact or diplomacy when it comes to employee management and people skills, and that his command tends toward the authoritarian. Yet when he wants a cleaner work area, the multimillionaire is not above picking up empty soda cans himself.

Despite Spike's fiddlings, the script is, for the most part, a strong and highly cinematic compression of an unwieldy book. Operating out of sequence, it takes some liberties in shifting time around, usually to some dramatic purpose. But not always. In one of the prison scenes, Spike has grafted onto Baldwin's fine work a gratuitous and jarring flash-forward to the present day. Malcolm's cellmate, Bembry, is asking Malcolm if the reason he straightens his hair is to make him look less black. Now, everyone knows that hair-straightening by Blacks was not just a phenomenon of the 1950s, but continues today. Yet Spike doesn't trust us to make the connection between then and now for ourselves; he's got to club us over the head with it, Louisville Slugger style. At this point in the script, Spike has scribbled:

CLOSE ON JERRI-CURLED MAN AND WOMAN WITH A WEAVE—1991 (TIME IS TODAY) Both are wearing blue/green contact lenses.

For all but the developmentally arrested, this point had been made more than adequately back in the cell.

Similarly, at another point Spike wants to cut to:

YOUNG AFRO-CENTRIC TEENAGERS WITH MALCOLM X T-SHIRTS, HATS, JACKETS, JEWELRY, ETC.

He even made a note to try to acquire the rights to insert a clip from Scorsese's 1988 *The Last Temptation of Christ* (featuring the blue-eyed Willem Dafoe) into a discussion of the Savior's skin tone.

Why shove the 1990s into a movie about someone who died in the 1960s? "To add relevance to today," would undoubtedly be his answer. But Malcolm's story *is* relevant to today; if it weren't, nobody would want to film it. The conclusion is inescapable: Spike doesn't think his audience is smart enough to figure these things out for themselves.

Elsewhere in those pages, Spike's instructions are merely baffling. In what is supposed to be concise directions for his cast and crew to follow, Spike has typed, "Black people still struggling to stay afloat in a racist white America that does not have their best interests at hand—8 years of Reagan and now at least 4 years of Bush." If Ernest Dickerson can capture all *that* in a single shot, he is truly a genius of the lens. In other words, what's good about the script is usually the work of James Baldwin and Arnold Perl, and what's bad about it is unmistakably the work of Spike Lee.

Fortunately, not all Spike's interruptions are so wrongheaded. When Malcolm X was buried, the actor Ossie Davis delivered a moving and much-quoted eulogy at his funeral. Naturally, as Spike has worked with Davis before, it was only appropriate that he have the actor read it again on the soundtrack in the aftermath of the assassination sequence.

Everyone knows that Malcolm, like Ghandi and JFK before him, was shot to death. It's what Spike has written *after* the assassination that's questionable. Other than Ossie Davis's eulogy, the final minutes are less denouement than anti-climax. After 200 pages of high drama, Spike dissolves to didactic preachiness and a we-are-the-world finale featuring Nelson Mandela and South African schoolchildren that is as sickeningly sentimental as anything in Spielberg's *Hook*. For hardheaded political drama suddenly to give way to such obvious guff raises serious questions about a director's artistic instincts.

Spike has described filming *Malcolm*'s climactic assassination scene at the Audubon Ballroom in Harlem as the most painful thing he has ever had to do. Watching Denzel-as-Malcolm getting shot over and over in take after take was not a pleasant experience for anyone. While in the area, Spike also took the opportunity to have Columbia University double for Harvard, and shot outdoor scenes of Malcolm lecturing to college students. He even did some filming in a Muslim restaurant the slain leader used to frequent on Lenox Avenue (now officially renamed Malcolm X Avenue, further evidence of Malcolm's current status).

Given the generous quantities of controversy and genuine ill-will that Spike has managed to provoke in his few years as a nationally recognized figure, there are many important people who would like nothing better than for him to fall flat on his face. On his most ambitious and expensive project, the ever-scrutinized Spike was subject to unprecedented levels of gossip. Throughout prep, production and postproduction of *Malcolm X*, the rumor mill would not stop grinding.

Warner Brothers knew it wanted to get behind *X*, but Spike, coproducer Monty Ross and line producer John Kilik found the $18 million shooting budget the studio was offering just too tight. The three knew what they needed was more like $34 million. To make up the shortfall, they sold foreign rights to Larry Gordon's Largo organization for an additional $8.5 million. But it still wasn't enough.

The Completion Bond Company, a Century City, California, completion-guarantee investment firm, then came through with the last few millions to make sure the film actually got finished—totalling $33.5 million. *Malcolm X*, Spike insisted to the *New York Post* "was never over budget, because we always knew it was going to cost that much. We knew it was going to cost more than we had . . . but it was a film I felt had to be made, and I had the opportunity to make it, so I did." Still, stories of Spike's extravagance would not go away. One vital statistic that may have been worrying the backers was that $33.5 million was $1.5 more than any Spike Lee movie had ever grossed at the North American box office!

Having heard these rumors that *X* was over budget, the *New York Post*'s Page Six talk-of-the-town specialists called Spike to confirm or deny. Instead of a news story, they got an impromptu editorial from a man on a very short fuse: "The *Post*," blurted Spike, "is a motherfucking racist rag and I hate it!" Click. Bzzzz. (Strangely, later that month, Spike sent the *Post* a Christmas card offering "Peace.")

In December, the bomb dropped. It became the industry's worst-kept secret that the Completion

Bond Company had exercised its right to take control over *Malcolm X*. Although many movies go over budget, the Bond Company resorts to the drastic action of taking over very few of them. What all this meant to Spike was that he would have to submit to the firm's wishes throughout the rest of the production and postproduction periods. He would not lose his fiercely guarded right to final cut, but would still have to do what the Bond Company wanted in the way of keeping costs under control. The Company would, they said, "keep him on a financial short rein" throughout postproduction. It wasn't that they didn't believe in Spike's vision of a *Malcolm* for the masses, but they did feel he had been profligate in his spending and needed to do some economizing.

Spike did his best to play down the importance of this undesirable development. Quietly, he volunteered much of his own $3 million salary to be used for closing the gap between the film's official and unofficial budgets. "Films go over budget all the time. We're looking for another investor. I'm not happy about it," Spike said in January 1992, "but I'm not letting it concern me." *Malcolm* may have been in disarray, but Spike still found time to honor a previous commitment to make a video for "Money Don't Matter 2 Night," one of those socially conscious songs Prince occasionally pens about the world beyond his groin.

Meanwhile, Spike and Denzel held a party to celebrate reaching the half-way point in the shooting.

With Christmas over, Spike prepared for another first in his brief but eventful life: shooting in a foreign country. In January, Spike flew to Cairo,

Egypt, to oversee the first Western film crew given permission to shoot the holy pilgrimage to Mecca. The pilgrimage—which inspired Malcolm to denounce his previous black supremacist philosophy and is therefore integral to the story—is something strictly off-limits to non-Muslims. Although deeply committed to his film, Spike was not quite willing to change his religion over it. There was, for a while, the rumor that Spike had had a conversion to Islam. The American Muslim movement's restrictions on smoking, drinking and drugs would not trouble the clean-living Spike, but the restrictions on sports, however, would: he couldn't live without his beloved Knicks.

Because of the Islamic code whereby "infidels" are banned from entering the holy city of Mecca, Spike could not personally participate in this particular part of his own film. Instead, he had to hand over the reins to second-unit technicians exclusively of the Muslim faith. Second units customarily handle such things as crowd scenes and travel footage, which require no real acting and thus no real directing. There was, therefore, nothing unusual about Spike not personally overseeing this segment of the shoot.

Spike, whose firsthand experience with the mother continent had been limited to one stay in Senegal, now experienced South Africa for the first time as he shot in the same, segregated, Soweto shantytown that Malcolm had himself toured some twenty-eight years earlier. While there, he filmed a segment with African National Congress leader Nelson Mandela for the epilogue. Upon finishing the shoot, Spike condemned Soweto as "unbelievable, a ghetto and a concentration camp."

This is not exactly news to anyone who keeps up with the International section of the newspaper. So why did Spike go there? Only a year earlier, he had railed in *SPIN* magazine about American corporations that still maintain branch plants in South Africa and had made a big deal of closing his accounts at Citibank for dealing with an "enemy" state. With the perennial controversy surrounding the issue of American and European entertainers playing South Africa, it's worth asking why it's okay for Spike to shoot a film there while Linda Ronstadt, Queen and even Millie Jackson and Ray Charles are reprimanded for playing Sun City. Wouldn't a shantytown in, say, Zimbabwe—or a soundstage, for that matter—have done just as well as Soweto? If Spike has an answer for any of this, the public hasn't heard it.

Principal photography on *Malcolm X* wrapped in the last week of January. The sigh of relief Spike heaved was to be short lived. For to wrap a film is the end of one ordeal and the beginning of another: Spike then began the long and arduous task of editing and sound-mixing his longest film yet—and with Bond Company bean-counters looking over his shoulder.

On February 10, Alex Haley, author of *Roots* and *The Autobiography of Malcolm X*, died in Seattle at the age of seventy. Sadly, the great African-American author would not live to see the film version of his 1965 literary milestone.

Ideology and race aside, *Malcolm X* is a rare

opportunity to see an important story from African-American history on the big screen and witness an African-American director hurling into the really big leagues for the first time. It's a tall order for a short guy, but if anyone can pull it off, Spike Lee can.

Chapter 16

Conclusion:
Players on the Same Team

As early as 1986, Spike said in *Film Comment* magazine that he didn't want his 40 Acres and a Mule Filmworks to "be seen as the savior of black people, as far as films are concerned. That's what happened with Richard Pryor's Indigo film company [the first major black production company]. I'm not trying to right everything that's been wrong as far as film and black people are concerned for the last hundred years." And yet, that often appears to be exactly what he's been trying to do over these past few years: make every film as though it may be the last chance he'll ever get to speak, so he'd better blurt it out—hell, shout it out—*right now* while there's still time. It's precisely this urgency that makes Spike Lee films compelling and energetic, but it's also why they're always threatening to veer off into diatribes.

Perhaps by the time number eight or nine comes around he'll have gotten enough of his fury out of his system so he can address serious issues without blowing his top. Perhaps it's only right that he should have spent his first few films letting off steam—after all, there is a fair amount of steam in black America that needs to be let off. But after a while, he'll have to mature, moderate, and show more variety in his films. Even Public Enemy is going to run out of racial topics eventually. And nobody wants an Angry Young Man with a receding hairline.

After *Do the Right Thing*, Spike felt he could afford to make a mellower movie; *Mo' Better Blues* was the result. Just how mellow might Spike get? "Someday I'll do something like *Twins*," Spike has said. "The studios know this." But until then, he's got a few things to get off his chest—in fact, quite a few things.

"You really carry a burden as a black filmmaker," said Spike in a late 1980s *Daily News* interview. "There are so few black films that when you do one it has to represent every black person in the world." By the beginning of the 1990s, these comments were becoming obsolete, and no one could have been happier about this than Spike himself. As of 1992, Spike has most definitely arrived and it no longer looks like he'll have to carry that burden. Maybe now Spike can relax a little.

Then again, maybe not: there is now so much black film activity out there that Spike is no longer the only game in town. By setting a precedent for others, he has inadvertently created competition for himself. Now that everybody's getting into the act, could Spike himself become obsolete? By inspiring a host of other, younger black filmmakers, Spike Lee may have created a Frankenstein's monster.

So what's in store for Spike now that he's not out there all alone? A record nineteen black-themed films were released in 1991, and a pleasingly diverse bunch they are–including *Boyz N the Hood*, *Straight Out of Brooklyn*, *The Five Heartbeats*, *Chameleon Street*, *Strictly Business*, *Livin' Large*, and *House Party 2*.

John Singleton (*Boyz*) in particular shows enormous promise. He was, after all, nominated for a Best Director Oscar—something still denied to Spike—becoming the first African-American so honored by the Academy. And Matty Rich's youth makes Spike look like the elder statesman of black film. (In fact, that title belongs more to men like Melvin Van Peebles, Bill Duke and Charles Burnett.) Perhaps *A Rage in Harlem* director Bill Duke said it best in early 1992 as his *Deep Cover* was about to be released: "We're all different players on the same basketball team."

Spike Lee has some serious competition out there now—not all of it friendly—and audiences have more choices of how to look at black life. Spike Lee's view, though the dominant one so far, is still only one opinion. Just as Spike himself has claimed that the black audience is not monolithic but varied, the same applies to the interpretations of their lives that those audiences want to see.

It's not hard to see Spike Lee as the man who made it possible for everyone from Robert Townsend (*Hollywood Shuffle, The Five Heartbeats*) to Charles

Lane (*Sidewalk Stories*, *True Identity*) to get started. And made it easier for black filmmakers to start at a reasonable level: Spike made his first feature for under $200,000, but John Singleton was handed $6 million for *Boyz N the Hood* (by Columbia, the company that turned down *Do the Right Thing* and showed little faith in *School Daze*).

Young Mr. Singleton then stepped smartly from *Boyz* into the extended, expensive music video "Remember the Time" for Michael Jackson, starring Eddie Murphy and Iman. It's safe to assume that, however happy Spike may be for Singleton's success, it's only natural that he also harbors a certain resentment for the (comparatively) smooth road Singleton has had to travel.

Despite the snub, when March 30, 1992 rolled around, Spike flew to Los Angeles and pinned a red AIDS-awareness ribbon onto one lapel of his tuxedo and his familiar Malcolm X pin onto the other. Nervously, Spike read from the TelePrompTer as he and the ubiquitous John Singleton presented the Best Documentary Oscars.

In early 1992, Spike told *Entertainment Weekly* of his desire to get one of his films—preferably, *Do the Right Thing*—issued on a Criterion laserdisc, complete with his own narration on the disc's second audio channel. MCA/Universal, however, didn't feel the smallish, connoisseur-oriented Criterion company could pay enough for the rights. With stinging irony, Criterion did issue special collector's editions of two other movies which have caused trouble for Spike Lee in the past: his 1989 Cannes nemesis *sex, lies and videotape*; and his 1991 box-office rival *Boyz N the Hood*.

In one of Spike's earliest interviews, Nelson George asked him if he'd like to be Steven Spielberg—that is, free not just to direct his own films but to oversee and executive-produce other people's. Lee's answer: "If I could have the power that Spielberg has but not be Steven Spielberg, nobody would turn that down." In 1992, Spike Lee finally got his wish as he stepped into his new role as America's first black movie mogul.

Early in 1992, Spike made an announcement: after six movies in seven years, he'd like to take a bit of a break. He would therefore not be directing again for a while and would concentrate instead on using his clout to executive-produce other people's projects under the aegis of 40 Acres and a Mule. He reaffirmed that he feels his rightful place is as an independent filmmaker working with Hollywood money—as much as he'd like to see black entrepreneurs eventually controlling the distribution and marketing of their own product. "Until then, I'm gonna stick with the Hollywood system,'cause there's nothing like it in the world [for getting movies to the people who want to see them]."

As the year began, Spike Lee and his extended family were branching out into explored territory—not just with producing films, but with a new record company, 40 Acres and a Mule Musicworks. In January, *Juice*, the first feature by Spike's long-serving camera ace Ernest Dickerson, opened to heavy security, strong business, generally enthusiastic reviews—and a shooting at a theater in Chicago.

In February, Spike turned academic. At the beginning of the month, he delivered his fourth annual filmmaking seminar at the Brooklyn campus of Long Island University. Several hundred enthusiastic students, filmmakers, and wannabees showed up for words of wisdom from the master. Spike did some proselytizing on behalf of two recent, well-reviewed but little-seen black films: Julie Dash's first feature, *Daughters of the Dust*, and Wendell Harris's *Chameleon Street*. "We've got to support movies like these," he admonished his audience, "and that means in the theaters, not on tape. Seeing a movie once it's on tape doesn't help the filmmaker." (*Daughters of the Dust* would not be obscure for much longer, however; shortly thereafter, it began a long commercial run.)

At that same event, Spike advised against too much optimism about the so-called black-film boom. "It's not necessarily going to go on forever," he warned. "As soon as these films stop making money, that's it. Hollywood will stop investing. We're past the point now where people will show up to see a movie just because it's black."

Also, according to Spike, too many of those films were indistinguishable from one another: "Either Blaxploitation, or black youth comedies like *House Party* and *Livin' Large*." There is much more to black life than that, he insisted, encouraging the crowd "to show the diversity of the black experience." He had obviously been doing a lot of thinking about the subject.

Later that month, Spike further solidified his intellectual reputation with a series of guest-lectures on African-American cinema at Harvard University for the spring semester. Films in his course (every one of them post–1971) included Melvin van Peebles's *Sweet Sweetback's Baadasssss Song* (1971), Gordon Parks' *Shaft* (1971), Michael Schultz's *Cooley High* (1975), Spike's own *She's Gotta Have It* (1986), Reginald Hudlin's *House Party* (1990), Charles Burnett's *To Sleep with Anger* (1990), and John Singleton's *Boyz N the Hood* (1991), as well as two of the better black-themed pictures by white directors, Martin Ritt's *Sounder* (1972) and Paul Schrader's *Blue Collar* (1978).

"Hey, this is Harvard, man," scolded Spike, as one student brought a boom-box to class, blasting the *Jungle Fever* soundtrack. Spike described the situation as "more like a circus" than a class: the trouble was his course was massively overbooked— even though it was available only to students of Afro-American Studies and Visual and Environmental Studies. A further restriction: Spike refused to admit any Boston Celtics fans.

The first of the lectures was moved to the 1,200-seat Sanders Theater after it became apparent that there were far more students (and non-students) clamoring to get in than the sixty actually enrolled in Contemporary African-American Cinema 182. Despite proclaiming that "My class is a dictatorship," Spike's entree into academia was wildly popular. "It's an honor just for me to teach young students in film . . . but they're going to have to work, they're going to have to write papers, see films. No backsliding, no skating in this class." The media mobbed students for their opinions after classes, especially when Spike again refused to endorse King's philosophy of "the complete use of non-violence"—though he did take pains to point out that he was speaking strictly for himself.

In the May 1992 issue of *Premiere*, the magazine did its annual tally of Hollywood's 100 most inflential power brokers. Spike stayed about the same, moving down a (fairly meaningless) four places, from sixty-seven to seventy-one. *Premiere*'s assessment: "solid performance of *Jungle Fever* upstaged by *Boyz N the Hood* raves. Went a measly $5 million over budget on *Malcolm X*, and suddenly it was Hello, Mr. Completion Bond people. Give him some slack, willya?"

Unfortunately, the sense of humor that Spike plies so effectively in his movies rarely surfaces in his sometimes self-righteous interviews. Because of this tendency to seriousness, a very funny man often comes across as sullen and irony-impaired. Some even feel he's at risk of becoming something absolutely fatal to any artist, and that is a bit of a bore. "I don't know where he's going with his movies," says a colleague. "I think he really believes in revenge, and revenge is not enough of a reason to be an artist. I'd like to see more of an internal quest. Is he going to grow as an artist and as a political thinker, or is he just going to repeat his same themes over and over for the rest of his life?"

On the personal front, Spike seems in no hurry to get married. His relationship with his *Jungle Fever* costar and model-actress Veronica Webb now over, "Being married would help free up a lot of time for Spike," says one who knows him well. "He's a busy, busy guy. When he's not making movies, he's doing videos, or he's starting a record company, or he's campaigning for Jesse, or he's at a Knicks game." And although Spike certainly has an eye for beautiful women, "He doesn't have *time* to go chasing a lot of girls."

Spike himself has said he'd like a marriage like his friends Ossie Davis and Ruby Dee have, a forty-five-year partnership in both life and art. As for children, he told *Playboy*, "When I do have a family, I don't want to send them to private school, because I feel that's too sheltered. I will be able to get my kids in the best public schools here. I mean, there are good public schools here, but there aren't that many. People are getting shot and stabbed in school. That's not supposed to happen in a school."

He's right to be concerned about the quality of life in New York City in the 1990s. For his part, Spike has done perhaps more than anyone to help transform Fort Greene to a vibrant, creative neighborhood drawing to Brooklyn talents (Branford Marsalis, for instance) who might otherwise take Manhattan. "It's a community rising," says Spike, "rising out of frustration." Spike would rather spend his free time there among his own people (or with his sports friends like Patrick Ewing, Magic, Michael Jordan and, until his imprisonment, "Brooklyn's own" Mike Tyson) than at Beverly Hills parties. Because of his refusal to go Hollywood—either geographically or psychologically—Spike seems pleasantly unchanged by success. Compare, for instance, his humble, work-oriented East Coast life to that of Eddie Murphy, who has enclosed himself in traditional star style with all the usual guards, gates and electronics between himself and his fans. The survival of Spike Lee as one of the pre-eminent forces in the North American media depends more than anything on keeping his ego in check.

As Spike himself has often pointed out, racism is America's number one issue, and somebody's got to bring it up. As Hollywood has a habit of ignoring or mishandling the tough topics, someone who can put meaningful issues on the screen and make them entertaining deserves not just attention but congratulations. Few living Americans have done more to get race on the national agenda than Spike Lee. When Spike says, "Wake up!", he's not only talking to Blacks. But a walk through any ghetto only confirms that there's still much work to be done. "I don't think any white folks have anything to fear from me," Spike once said. Instead, he's just "doing what makes me the happiest, that's making films."

Looking to the future—despite all his multi-faceted grief over *Malcolm X*—Spike Lee feels no need to hesitate. "I'm not scared," he insists. "We don't intend to drop the ball." Well, he'd better not, because in an industry where you're only as hot as your last picture, one failure could undo much of the good work Spike has accomplished over the past decade. Disturbing events everywhere from Crown Heights to Louisiana voting booths indicate that racism is alive and well—and maybe even on the rise. As long as that is the case, the world will still need the movies of Spike Lee.

ALEX PATTERSON was born in Toronto, Canada, in 1958. He has an Honors B.A. from York University in Toronto (Sociology major, English minor). He has written about film and related subjects for *Premiere*, *The Village Voice*, *Film Comment*, *The Toronto Star* and *The Globe and Mail*, and is the film critic for Toronto's *eye Weekly*.

Mr. Patterson lives in the great borough of Brooklyn, New York.